A CLEVELAND LEGACY

A CLEVELAND LEGACY

The Architecture of Walker and Weeks

ERIC JOHANNESEN

THE KENT STATE UNIVERSITY PRESS

KENT, OHIO, AND LONDON

In cooperation with The Western Reserve Historical Society

© 1999 by The Kent State University Press, Kent, Ohio 44242

All rights reserved

Library of Congress Catalog Card Number 97-36507

ISBN 0-87338-589-6

Manufactured in the United States of America

Published in cooperation with The Western Reserve Historical Society.

05   04   03   02   01   00   99   5   4   3   2   1

Frontispiece: Severance Hall, 1929–30.

Designed & composed in 11-point Electra by Diana Dickson and
Will Underwood at The Kent State University Press.
Printed & bound by Thomson-Shore, Inc.

LIBRARY OF CONGRESS CATALOGING-IN-PUBLICATION DATA
Johannesen, Eric.
     A Cleveland legacy : the architecture of Walker and Weeks /
     Eric Johannesen.
          p.   cm.
     Includes bibliographical references and index.
     ISBN 0-87338-589-6 (cloth : alk. paper) ∞
     1. Walker and Weeks (Firm) 2. Walker, Frank R. 3. Weeks, Harry E.
4. Architecture—Ohio—Cleveland. 5. Architecture, Modern—20th
century—Ohio—Cleveland. 6. Cleveland (Ohio)—Buildings, structures,
etc. I. Title.
NA737.W264J66   1998
720'.92'2—dc21   97-36507

British Library Cataloging-in-Publication data are available.

CONTENTS

FOREWORD

Through a fortuitous series of events and actions, the Western Reserve Historical Society Library became the repository for an immense archive of the Cleveland architectural firm of Walker and Weeks. Responding to a call in 1975 to "Come and get them," without time to conduct the customary review and selection, the staff decided to take all the records of the original Walker and Weeks from the basement of the Osborn Medical Building, where they had been accumulating dust for many years and were about to be discarded. Van-loads of transfer file cases, drawings and blueprints, and photographs were moved to the Library's off-site records center. There, the collection, which ultimately consisted of 450 linear feet of files and 250 cubic feet of rolled drawings, reposed until it was moved to the Library's new building when it opened in 1984.

With the collection accessible, Eric Johannesen, with the assistance of two archival interns, surveyed the files and drawings. Their discoveries convinced him that Walker and Weeks was worthy of a scholarly study, and he began to focus his talent and energy on this project. In January 1989 Eric wrote a proposal for a publication that "would serve as a monograph on the firm and a catalog to the collection. . . . The emphasis may not be so much on the biography of the principals in the firm as on the projects, their clients, and the place of this architecture in the first half of the twentieth century."

Eric Johannesen was the right person for this job. As the Historical Society's preservationist since 1973, he became expert in historic preservation and local architectural heritage. He inventoried historic structures throughout Northeast Ohio and nominated buildings for the National Register of Historic Places. This work was capped in 1979 by the publication of his classic *Cleveland Architecture 1876–1976*.

Eric completed the Walker and Weeks manuscript shortly before he died, unexpectedly, in 1990. His coworkers and friends at the Historical Society, with the encouragement and support of his brothers, Rolf and Donald Johannesen, agreed to see that his manuscript on Walker and Weeks was published. John J. Grabowski reviewed the manuscript and served as liaison between the Historical Society and the publisher, The Kent State University Press. Drew Rolik helped to edit the manuscript and select the illustrations suggested by Johannesen's notes.

But the work is that of Eric Johannesen. In his memory, which we cherish, we are pleased to present *A Cleveland Legacy: The Architecture of Walker and Weeks*.

Kermit J. Pike
Western Reserve Historical Society

INTRODUCTION

I N THE SUMMER OF 1930, the first issue of the journal *Architectural Re-vue of the Mississippi Basin* was published in Columbus, Ohio. The entire publication was devoted to the work of Walker and Weeks and contained 170 illustrations. The publisher's introductory note stated that "Walker & Weeks have been selected for the introductory number because of their prominence and the fine character of the work they have done in Ohio, Indiana and the Middle-West. . . . the firm of Walker & Weeks is recognized as being instrumental to a large degree, in the development of a fine style of architecture in the Mid-West."[1] Inasmuch as there were no more issues of the *Revue*, and in spite of the fact that it was the beginning of the Great Depression, it is possible that this "issue" was a promotional piece of a type not uncommon in the period. Nevertheless, there is no gainsaying the fact that Walker and Weeks was the foremost architectural firm in the city of Cleveland for nearly forty years between 1911 and 1949. As the architects of the major classical public buildings in Cleveland of the 1920s and 1930s, their names are well known. However, few people are familiar with their work from a prolific decade prior to 1920, with the large number of suburban residences and hundreds of lesser-known buildings designed by them, or with their regional reputation. After thirty years in business, Walker himself, making application for a city hall commission, cataloged work that included:

> general layout work (private and public, city planning), public and [corporate] buildings of various kinds, involving architectural design, structural engineering and special engineering, viz., mechanical apparatus, elevators and conveyors, heating and ventilating, electrical, cooling plants, insulating, etc.
>
> The variety of buildings included warehouses, office buildings (city and manufacturing plants), auditoriums, shops, fire stations, chemical laboratories, mass housing (municipal) and small unit housing, bridge, road and viaduct work, machine shops, swimming tanks and college groups.[2]

Although there is virtually no documentary evidence of Walker & Weeks's intentions in 1911, the body of their work, as well as their method, indicates that they must have proposed from the outset to establish an "architectural factory" of the type pioneered by Daniel Burnham in Chicago in the 1890s. A method developed by Burnham originally for the planning of the Columbian Exposition, and refined to deal with large corporate commissions, it comprised what William H. Jordy has called "barracks of draftsmen" integrated with "a corps of engineering and planning specialists."[3] Burnham's example was widely imitated across the country by firms such as McKim, Mead & White, the most prestigious early-twentieth-century American architects, and also continued by Burnham's successor firm Graham, Anderson, Probst & White. Jordy also points out in some detail how the methods of beaux-arts training provided the ideal background for such an organization. Its emphasis on the analysis of the fundamental plan requirements of the commission; their organization into a logical, coherent, and generally symmetrical composition; and the expression of the plan on the exterior facades was appropriate for a team operation. In spite of the beaux-arts emphasis on tradition, correct models, and symmetrical compositional patterns, the method left open the choice of style, the possibility of combining details eclectically, and even the creation of modern variations.

Twentieth-century artistic criticism has long maintained the view of the architect as an individual creative artist whose primary concern is the making of a personal aesthetic statement. From the point of view of public need, however, the architect is a practitioner who provides shelter with practicality, economy, and good looks at a consistent level of quality. To this end, his or her practice is designed to analyze a need, to develop serviceable spaces and workable floor plans, and to provide an attractive envelope for these requirements. The better architects are those who bring to this practice a high degree of organization, imagination, and taste, and they have always been very few in number.

Because of the money and the building opportunities in the late nineteenth and early twentieth centuries, Cleveland attracted numerous good architects. In 1920 the *Cleveland City Directory* listed 120 architects, the great majority of which were small offices that could handle simple jobs and relied on consultants for mechanical and structural services. Walker and Weeks, however, was one of the few firms with a large organization that was prepared to manage every phase of a commission. Theirs was a completely integrated business capable of handling all aspects of design, construction, and mechanical work. By 1914 the young firm had undertaken more than $4 million worth of construction (1996–97 equivalent around $82 million) and had a permanent staff of thirty men. The partners developed a style of operation that enabled them to become the most successful architects in Cleveland. They seemed to have an unusual capacity for grasping an opportunity and developing a network of successful and influential clients. A 1914 article commending Walker and Weeks's combination of artistry and good business concluded that "Mr. Walker and Mr. Weeks have taught the most difficult lesson of all; that good architecture is, above all else, the fulfilling of needs. A building must be a distinctly artistic creation, but must also be a commercial and economic success and serve well the purposes for which it was designed."[4]

It is nearly impossible to speak of an architect's personal style in the early twentieth century. Paradoxically, the most characteristic architects of the period are not those whose style was idiosyncratic and easily identifiable but those whose work exhibits no common style. Walker and Weeks, however, is considered by many to have a recognizable style, mainly the neoclassic. Their academic beaux-arts training prepared them to address any design problem and to make plans in any of the historical idioms. Moreover, if a modern style was recognized as having value, it could easily become part of the classical architect's vocabulary. There was no inconsistency or lack of integrity in working with various styles of manners simultaneously. The style of a building was determined less by any discernible architectural philosophy than by its function or symbolism, the wishes of the builders, the type of site, the amount of money available, or the dictates of fashion.

chapter 1

WALKER AND WEEKS

Walker and Weeks began as the partnership of two young men from Massachusetts. Harry E. Weeks (1871–1935) was born in West Springfield on October 2, 1871. He attended the public schools there and then entered the Massachusetts Institute of Technology, graduating in 1893. He married Alice B. Tuggey in 1896. Weeks worked for several architectural firms in Massachusetts and had his own firm in Pittsfield for three years before coming to Cleveland in 1905 at the suggestion of John M. Carrere of the distinguished New York firm of Carrere & Hastings and a member of the Cleveland Group Plan commission.

Frank R. Walker (1877–1949) was born in Pittsfield on September 29, 1877. He proudly traced his family to the early seventeenth-century New England settlers in America. Walker's father was an interior decorator in Pittsfield, a profession that no doubt helped influence Frank's choice of architecture as a career. He attended the public schools of Pittsfield and graduated from the Massachusetts Institute of Technology in 1900. Walker spent more than a year studying in the atelier of a Monsieur Redon, followed by another year in Italy. Upon his return to the States, he worked in the office of Guy Lowell in Boston, the prominent architect of the Boston Museum of Fine Arts and the New York County Courthouse. Walker subsequently became Lowell's office manager in New York. After a brief time working in Pittsburgh, he also came to Cleveland in 1905 at the suggestion of Carrere. Both Walker and Weeks joined the office of J. Milton Dyer.

Dyer was a brilliant but uneven architect whose work in Cleveland covered an astonishing range, from the beaux-arts City Hall to the 1940 modernistic Coast Guard Harbor Station. However, for such important Dyer projects as the Cleveland Athletic Club, a remarkable tall building erected on the air rights above an existing structure in 1910–11, Walker was the principal designer and Weeks the job supervisor. And in later years Walker claimed credit for the design of Dyer's most important public buildings — the Cleveland City Hall, the Lake County Courthouse in Painesville, Ohio, and the Summit County Courthouse in Akron.[5] There

Walker, Weeks, and staff. Front row (*from left*): Frank R. Walker, Claude Stedman, H. F. Horn (?), and Dana Clark (?). Back row (*from left*): Harry E. Weeks, Byron Dalton, Armen Tashjian, and Dan Mitchell.

is also reason to believe that Walker may have been responsible for the major residences out of Dyer's office, the Edmund S. Burke and Lyman Treadway houses. In other works, Dyer's best work was done while Walker and Weeks were in his office, and his significant work after 1911 was negligible. According to acquaintances of Dyer, his social habits became more and more erratic, sometimes keeping him away from the office for days and even weeks at a time, and in 1911 and 1912 many of the younger men left him. In 1911 Walker and Weeks formed their own partnership and set up an office at 1900 Euclid Avenue.

The partnership of Walker and Weeks grew during a period of rapid urban growth and booming industry and later blossomed during the high finance and big business of the 1920s. Banks, offices, and commercial buildings dominated their work for much of their career. Walker and Weeks met the extraordinary demands of complexity and largeness of scale by developing their departmentalized organization. (In fact, many good-sized businesses had fewer employees than they did.) Their annual volume of construction during the twenties was between $5 and $10 million (perhaps $102–$204 million in 1996–97).

In the heyday of the 1920s, the staff numbered sixty and there were eight partners in the firm. Besides Frank Walker and Harry Weeks, there were Claude Stedman, designer; Armen Tashjian, chief engineer; Byron Dalton, salesman and bank contact; Dana Clark, designer; H. F. Horn, later to be officer manager; J. Byers Hays, designer; Winifred Robblee, treasurer; and Dan Mitchell, chief draftsman and field supervisor. The office had its own staff photographer, Carl F. Waite. Other staff members were in charge of specification writing; drafting; structural, mechanical, and electrical engineering; architectural and construction details; field supervision; business management; and all of the manifold tasks required by the large firm.

According to Charles H. Stark, an architect who worked in the firm in the early 1930s, Walker and Weeks were "a strange combination."[6] Frank Walker, a big likable man, boisterous and sometimes earthy, was an excellent architect who knew good design. Harry Weeks was the "organizer in office politics" who kept the staff happy and together. Quiet and mild-mannered, a gentleman, who the men in the office always referred to as "Mr. Weeks," he was "never seen with a pencil in his hand," but he liked to stand at his office door and look out over the drafting room. Walker, on the other hand, came into the drafting room occasionally, sat down at someone's drawing board, and sketched a few suggestions for changes. The respective roles of Frank Walker and Harry Weeks were also described in the article that appeared in 1914: "Mr. Weeks has always been more particularly devoted to the structural and practical phases of architecture and the immediate success of the new firm is in no small measure due to this accurate knowledge of the many-sided duties devolving upon him. Mr. Walker, on the other hand, is a designer of rare ability, standing high in architectural circles, and a member of the American Institute of Architects."[7]

Most of Walker and Weeks's jobs were brought into the office by members of the firm. Partners or teams specializing in certain types of buildings sought out the clients. Each partner had special skills and was a good architect in his own right, but each also acted as salesman, covering his specialties, whether banks, churches, offices, or factories. The partners handled the business relations, correspondence, and meetings between Walker and Weeks and the clients. The phenomenon of "marketing" by architects has been thought of as a relatively recent one, but their use of this strategy, in addition to the offering of complete planning services, is certainly one of the keys to the extraordinary success of Walker and Weeks.

The design process in the office was outlined in a paper by Claude Stedman, which begins with the premise that "Almost all modern buildings, apart from dwellings, form the skeleton and the enclosing shell of some extremely complex industrial or commercial operating organization."[8] The architects began a series of conferences with the client in order to gather data on the requirements of the building and, in a complex operation, of various departments and their relationships with each other. The development of program requirements could take several months, after which the design team began to study the development of the plan, including such factors as placement on a site, relationship of exterior to interior, the separation and connection of various functions, and the mechanical and structural systems. Again, in a complex building the development of the plan could take many months.

After the basic plan was approved draftsmen and architects began preparing working drawings in ink on linen, which required different sets for general floor plans, structural work, heating and ventilating systems, plumbing, and electrical engineering. At the same time, the exterior design was evolved through studies, sketches, and, if necessary, plaster models. The design and working drawings were handled by the job crew familiar with the particular type of building. If presentation renderings were required, J. Byers Hays, Wilbur Adams, and an unnamed artist of German extraction executed them. This entire design process took weeks or months or even an entire year and the efforts of a small team of up to thirty men, including the designers, draftsmen, and engineers in all of the fields.

The architects wrote the detailed specifications for the taking of bids and oversaw the contractual work. When construction began, they worked with the general contractor and the various subcontractors, who prepared shop drawings, sometimes numbering in the thousands, which had to be checked, often several times, by the architects. At the construction site, the architect's field supervisor worked with the contractor on scheduling each task in order to avoid delays or conflicts among the subcontractors. This meant daily conferences, and frequently additional detail drawings were required.

The firm's method was further explained in a proposal prepared by Byron Dalton for the Libbey Glass Company:

> Our method of solving a problem such as the development of a plant of your type is perhaps different than that practiced by most architects and engineers. We could suggest the approaching of your problem in the following manner. To place our engineers and equipment men in your plant, working with the heads of various departments for your man in charge of construction and gathering all of the various requirements and details of

2341 Carnegie Building (Walker and Weeks office building), 1926.

every nature and then writing a program based on what we have found. We would then proceed to develop a plan reflecting your requirements so that your plant would operate in the most efficient manner.

On rare occasions we have found organizations that contain an individual who has at his finger tips all the information necessary upon which to base a program, but in most cases we have found it necessary to go to the various heads of departments. . . .

We retain a complete corps of engineers covering structural, both concrete and reinforcing, and all branches of mechanical work, which is quite exceptional except in organizations as large as ours, and we are sure that because of having these men within our own organization we can develop a much more homogeneous result than should it be necessary for us to call in various outside concerns to work in the different services which go to make up a complete building.

As to economical construction, our engineers and working drawing men have striven for years to keep down the cost of construction of our various types of building.[9]

For fifteen years Walker and Weeks's office was located on the eighth floor of the 1900 Euclid Building, and then in 1926 the firm moved into a six-story office building which they had designed, at 2341 Carnegie Avenue. They occupied 9,700 square feet on the fifth and sixth floors; they leased the ground floor to a Lincoln Motor Car dealer and the intermediate floors to other tenants. Behind the classical front, a factory-like concrete-frame structure allowed ample clerestory light into the large fifth-floor drafting room, which measured 40 by nearly 120 feet. Along the sides of the room were the separate offices for designers, artists, the engineering department, specification writers, executives, and bookkeeping. The plan of Walker and Weeks's office was described in *The American Architect* as being a direct expression of the operation of the firm:

> Each job or commission is placed in charge of an executive and a designer with a job captain and suitable corps of draftsmen. Insofar as conditions permit, to simplify administration of the work, the six designers' offices are located opposite those of the executives in charge, with the drafting force for the job between them. Contrary to the method employed in many large offices of keeping drawings in a file room in charge of a clerk, all drawings are maintained in files in the drafting room and made readily accessible to the executives, designers and draftsmen.[10]

There were three conference rooms for client meetings, and a library (20 x 40 feet) for the collection of historical style reference books that were constantly consulted by an academic architect. There were also sample rooms of materials used by both staff and the clients. For example, the marble and tile sample room was completely lined with 9-x-12-inch marble slabs, comprising what was called probably the most complete collection of marble samples in the country, and the floor was composed of various kinds, patterns, and sizes of tile. Similarly, the window openings in the offices were fitted with different types of frames and sashes for inspection by clients. On the sixth floor were Walker's 30-foot-long studio, a roof terrace, a bath, a storage vault, and a balcony overlooking the drafting room. In addition, there was a private dining room that seated about twenty; the staff signed up in the morning for lunch seating, the partners of the firm and employees with the most seniority having first choice.

The size of the organization meant that the firm often had dozens of commissions in the office at the same time, and the projects were allotted to the various designers. Among the chief designers were Dana L. Clark, Claude W. Stedman, J. Byers Hays, Edwin J. Truthan, and Elmer Babb. One designer could be responsible for the functional layout and another for the architectural elevations. Clark remained in the firm for thirty-five years and became head of architectural design, and Stedman, with Walker and Weeks for the entire life of the firm, beginning in 1914 became head of planning design. Nevertheless, according to Stark, Frank Walker maintained control and final approval of all work produced by the office.

Frank Walker himself clearly viewed the business of architecture as more than the designing of buildings. He saw it as the opportunity for shaping a whole environment, making architecture became a full-time professional activity. He was employed by the Cleveland City Plan Commission as its first professional adviser and collaborated with Robert H. Whitten in that capacity from 1918 to 1928. He was a member of the City Plan Commission for ten years when its principal work included studying the role of city planning in other cities and preparing a city plan for Cleveland, overseeing the development of the public works and Daniel Burnham's Mall plan, and improving the streets and platting. Beginning in 1918 Walker was also an active member of the city plan committee of the Cleveland Chamber of Commerce. This committee reviewed public improvements, such as hospitals and public bath house designs, and promoted city and countywide schemes for rationalizing urban development, such as establishing local planning commissions, accepting land-use zoning, and adopting a uniform platting ordinance for Cuyahoga County.

Walker was interested in several undertakings in connection with what he called "pedagogical work related to architecture."[11] In 1921, when he was president of the Cleveland chapter of the American Institute of Architects, a group of architects led by Walker, Abram Garfield (son of President James A. Garfield), and others began a course in architecture at the Cleveland School of Art, which became the Cleveland School of Architecture in 1924. Walker served as a trustee of the school and a member of the faculty. The architects supported it financially until it became part of Western Reserve University in 1929.

Walker also acted as critic and patron of an atelier that became part of the John Huntington Polytechnic Institute in 1918. The institute was a technical night school that offered free instruction to "deserving persons

. . . who are unable to acquire a collegiate education."[12] The students, required to be employed in one of the applied arts or an industrial occupation, were offered courses in architecture, industrial design, and structural engineering.

In 1927 Walker and Garfield were chosen as architectural advisers to a University Circle Planning Commission. They were assigned the task of developing a master plan and an architectural scheme that would be the foundation of future developments in University Circle, the cultural center that is home to a host of institutions, including the Cleveland Museum of Art, the Cleveland Orchestra, and Case Western Reserve University.

Finally, Walker played a key role in the revival and transformation of the suburban village of Gates Mills after he settled there in 1915.

chapter 2

RESIDENCES

I N 1910 CLEVELAND had just climbed to sixth place among the cities of
the United States. As an industrial metropolis and transportation hub,
Cleveland had many monied residents, and there seemed to be limitless
opportunities to build. Vast personal fortunes were still being made. (The
power of Congress to levy taxes on income did not pass until 1913.) For
these wealthy and influential clients, Walker and Weeks designed buildings of virtually every type. Although the extravagant expenditure for
mansions of the likes of Cleveland's Sylvester Everett, Samuel Andrews,
and Charles Brush in the 1880s had run its course, there were many who
aspired to large and comfortable, if not palatial, houses. The social and
economic classes were still defined in a way that is difficult for present-
day readers to conceive of. There were clear-cut social distinctions, from
old families to the newly prosperous to solid business and professional
men, and these differences were expressed in their homes.

Residences comprised by far the largest group of Walker and Weeks's
early commissions and included "cottages," upper-middle-class houses,
and one or two mansions. All of them were characteristic of the trends of
the time in residential design. The first decade of the century had been a
period of transition and experiment, and the interior plan that had been
developing since the late nineteenth century came into full flowering. A
desire for practical, more informal modern living replaced the ostenta-
tion of the Gilded Age. Homeowners wanted economy both in the use of
space and in the operation of the home. An impression of spaciousness
was achieved by large openings between rooms. The entrance hall, still
an important circulation feature, was no longer the main reception room.
A living room replaced the Victorian parlor and was designed to be comfortable for a grouping of people, with a fireplace as the focus. Next to the
living room there was frequently an attached enclosed piazza or sun porch.
Across the hall from the living room was the dining room. Somewhere
there was a room serving the need for privacy—study, den, or library.
Finally, a well-to-do, upper-middle-class household was run and supported
by at least three servants, usually a maid, a cook, and a laundress, and the

George N. Sherwin residence, Cleveland Heights, 1912.

house included living quarters for them. (There was a plentiful supply of domestic help among poor immigrant girls.)

The architect's problem was the grouping of these areas, and this was done with a keen regard for their orientation to the out-of-doors. As for style, echoes of the late 1800s remained, especially from the shingle style. There was a mixture of style sources; in fact, the dominant mode was a general eclecticism. Neoclassic, Georgian, Tudor, and Jacobean elements were freely used. It should also be remembered that wages for workmen and the cost of building materials were vastly cheaper than they became in the second half of the century, a factor that encouraged fine detail work.

Most of the residential work for Cleveland architects in the teens was in the Wade Park subdivision near Western Reserve University or the grow-

F. W. Judd residence, Shaker Heights, 1912.

ing suburbs of Cleveland Heights and Shaker Heights. The first recorded residential commission for Walker and Weeks in 1911 was one of a series for a new development called Carlton Park. Carlton Road, a pleasant cul-de-sac branching off Overlook Road on the promontory of the Heights (today it leads to the dormitory towers of Case Western Reserve University), was just a few steps from the Euclid Heights streetcar on Cedar Road. Euclid Heights, now a part of Cleveland Heights, was very much a streetcar suburb, for the horse-drawn carriage and the streetcar were still the most common modes of transportation, for the automobile was considered a plaything of the rich man. Many Euclid Heights residents had automobiles, which were usually stabled in a detached carriage house, though several of Walker and Weeks's Carlton Road houses had attached garages, which must have been among the earliest appearances in Cleveland of this feature.

The young firm designed at least six of the thirteen houses on Carlton Road. Among others, the little enclave was occupied by George N. Sherwin, a vice president of the Union Trust Company; Ermine Barrows Jones, the widow of James M. Jones, a common pleas judge, and her daughter Myrta L. Jones, noted social reformer and women's activist; and

BOULEVARD·ELEVATION
¼"=1'-0"

Max McMurray residence, Bratenahl, 1914.

Mrs. Henry L. Sanford, a founder of the Women's City Club. The houses were all medium-sized suburban homes of shingle or wooden clapboard siding with steep, sheltering gable roofs. The main facades were individualized by unsymmetrically placed windows and small jogs and wings in the plan and here and there a columned portico, a recessed entry portico, a bay window, or a sun porch with stubby stucco columns. All the floor plans were similar, with a central entrance hall and room arrangements that were variations on the domestic plans described above. Although modest by the standards of the previous generation's mansions on Euclid Avenue's "Millionaires' Row," the Carlton Road houses—with their large living areas, three or four bedrooms, and the servants' quarters—were not small.

Another class of residences was somewhat larger and was characterized by a more emphatic, not to say massive, hip roof that was brought down over a porch in the contemporary bungalow fashion. These homes were often brick. The prototype was the one planned for F. W. Judd on Marlboro Road in Cleveland Heights in 1912, where the sloping roof rests on a brick arcade on the outdoor terrace or porch, and a smaller version was built for Oliver Renkert of Canton. Still another type—prefigured by the Edmund Burke residence (Cleveland Music School Settlement) that was done by Dyer's office in 1909–10—had a facade framed by two gables. The finest of these was the stucco house built for James H. Foster on Devonshire Drive in Ambler Heights, and its form could be seen as a direct reference to the work of contemporary English architect C. F. A. Voysey, who was working in a revival of a country vernacular idiom.

In 1913–14 Walker and Weeks were also fortunate to get commissions for two genuine mansions. The first was built for Benedict Crowell, assistant secretary of war under Newton D. Baker and president of Crowell-Lundoff Construction. Erected on Magnolia Drive in Wade Park, the Crowell house was a large stucco mansion in the Renaissance style with a balustraded cornice. Its long narrow floor plan included six bedrooms, extensive servants' quarters, and a side porte-cochere entrance. The second mansion was built in Bratenahl for Max McMurray, the general manager of furnaces for the United Iron and Steel Company. Similar in style to Crowell's, his house was a large stucco classical villa. Some of the features, such as an arcaded veranda, have a decidedly Mediterranean air, perhaps befitting its lakeside site. Although the Crowell house was razed for the construction of the Veterans Administration Hospital, the McMurray mansion is still standing.

It is not surprising that the fledgling firm also had a number of remodeling jobs — anything from making simple, practical changes to transforming houses with a late-Victorian flavor into a more fashionable classical look. These jobs were not limited to Cleveland and its suburbs; Walker and Weeks took on remodeling projects elsewhere in Ohio as well as in other states. They even performed work on the flamboyant Long Island residence of Raymond Hitchcock, a prominent stage actor who was the contemporary of Lillian Russell and George M. Cohan, although the reason for a commission so far away is not recorded.

But Frank Walker also received a number of commissions for small houses and for the remodeling of some nineteenth-century Greek revival houses in the country village of Gates Mills, about twelve miles from downtown Cleveland. Gates Mills is where, in October 1915, Walker and his bride, Katharine Tollett Stone, made their home. He became one of the prime movers in restoring and developing the rural retreat. The bustling nineteenth-century milltown had quieted into a sleepy village by the 1890s. It was rediscovered by business and professional men from Cleveland who saw that its beautiful valley setting and New England character would make an ideal residential area. The leaders formed the Maple Leaf Land Company, which made improvements to the roads, bridges, fences, and buildings and built the Cleveland and Eastern Railway, an electric interurban line that connected downtown Cleveland with Gates Mills, Chardon, and Burton and began operation in 1900. The nineteenth-century houses were restored and renovated as summer homes. A picturesque New England style was promoted and controlled. All houses were painted white. In 1905 the Gates Mills Improvement Society was incorporated to improve the property and foster the well-being of the community. Walker served as president of the Improvement Society from 1917 to 1919 and was instrumental in the village's incorporation in 1920, after which he was elected mayor and served two terms, 1921–24. Those who knew him reported that his administrative ability and firm conviction that the village should maintain its New England traditions enabled him to organize a local government that involved the participation of citizens in all departments.

Sooner or later Walker worked on the homes of the founders and most of the important residents of the new village: S. Prentiss Baldwin, a retired lawyer whose ornithological research facility at Gates Mills was among the first to make a scientific approach to the study of bird migration; Frank H. Ginn, a lawyer in the firm of Tolles, Hogsett, Ginn & Morley and counselor to the fabled Van Sweringens; Crispin Oglebay, president of Ferro Machine and later of Oglebay-Norton; A. A. Augustus, a coal mining executive and member of the Council of National Defense in 1917; A. C. Ernst, founder of the Ernst & Ernst accounting firm; and Francis Drury, whose Gates Mills house later became the home of Gilmour Academy.

In the vicinity of Gates Mills, neighboring Orange Township (now Hunting Valley), and across the county line, some of Cleveland's wealthiest established large country estates that were representative of the social pretensions of the era. The pattern in many of the assignments was to erect small utilitarian buildings first, with a cottage for temporary residence, and then to add the grand estate house at a later date. The earliest of these commissions consisted of buildings planned in 1914 for Andrew Squire, founder of Squire, Sanders and Dempsey, at his Valleevue Farm in Hunting Valley. The principal farm building was a classically detailed U-shaped barn with cattle stalls, hayloft, and tool and wagon rooms. Among the largest estates were Howard M. Hanna Jr.'s farm in Kirtland and Walter C. White's Circle W Farm (now Hawken School) in Chester Township, Geauga County.

Walker and Weeks supervised the planning and design of the entire estate between 1917 and 1924. White's wealth was generated by industry, his family having founded the White Sewing Machine Company and then the White Motor Company. Like some other industrialists of his generation, White created a working farm, with cultivated acres, a dairy herd, orchards, formal gardens, and polo fields, where the lord of the manor could play seriously at being a country gentleman. The main house is Georgian revival or colonial in style, with a pillared and balustraded portico like Mount Vernon. A glassed-in porch at one end was carried over from the domestic plan of the suburban houses closer to the city. An ell is an extensive gambrel-roofed servants' wing with dormers, a six-car garage, porte-cochere, and an attached greenhouse. To the east of the house the main entrance drive crosses a small triple-arched masonry

Walter C. White residence, Gates Mills, 1917.

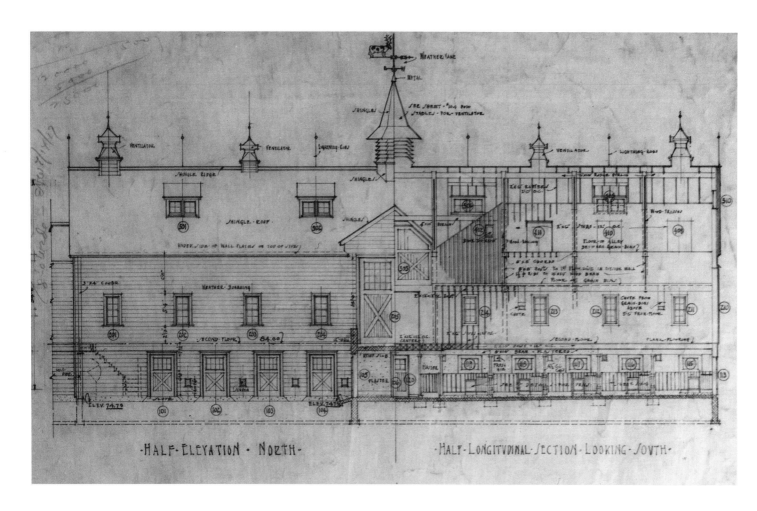

One of several barns on the Walter C. White
estate, Gates Mills, 1917.

bridge. Walker and Weeks designed similar rustic, medieval-style stone bridges for several other country estates, and they were built by a local stonemason, George Brown.

Not far from the White house is a U-shaped polo stable, very simple in style with steep gable roofs and faced in stucco. A hunt hall and stablemaster's house are attached, and beyond the stable is a small lodge in the same style. One of the major buildings of the estate, the vast, sprawling dairy barn, was destroyed by fire in 1977. The enormous T-shaped complex had a great gambrel-roofed core and two giant tile silos. Almost factory-like, a long gabled wing with turreted ventilators ran across the ridge, and a picturesque gate house led into the barnyard. To that extent, the barn complex was an expression both of romantic rural nostalgia and up-to-date scientific efficiency. The same could be said of the entire conception of a modern working farm with colonial plantation architecture and feudal set pieces.

Throughout the twenties, Walker continued to shape physically the Village of Gates Mills. In 1926 the Methodist Church ceded the little 1835 meetinghouse that had been built by Holsey Gates, which was noted for its mixture of Greek and gothic detail, and transferred it to the Episcopal Church. Renamed St. Christopher's-by-the-River, it was restored and remodeled for the Episcopal service by Walker. He lengthened the church with a chancel and added a new pulpit, altar, and lectern. Walker's generally classical inclination brought about an appropriate and complementary solution. In 1929 the village built a townhall designed by Walker and Weeks, a two-story brick building with a obligatory colonial belfry and columned front stoop and, underneath, a garage for the fire engine.

The restoration of Gates Mills was a syntheses of historic re-creation and corporate management. The creation of the image of a colonial village was a carefully managed stage effect. The New England character was achieved and enhanced by financial investment, gentlemen's agreements, zoning and building restrictions, and the presence of a major classical architect in Frank Walker.

In Cleveland and its immediate suburbs, many of Walker and Weeks's more than three dozen residential commissions in the late teens followed the informal plan and outline of the first decade of the century, with hints of the bungalow, prairie, or arts and crafts styles. Others began to tend toward a more archaeological revival, in which the stylistic details were less freely adapted and more strictly taken from historical precedent. Two examples of each tendency may suffice. Not surprisingly, all of them were designed for business executives.

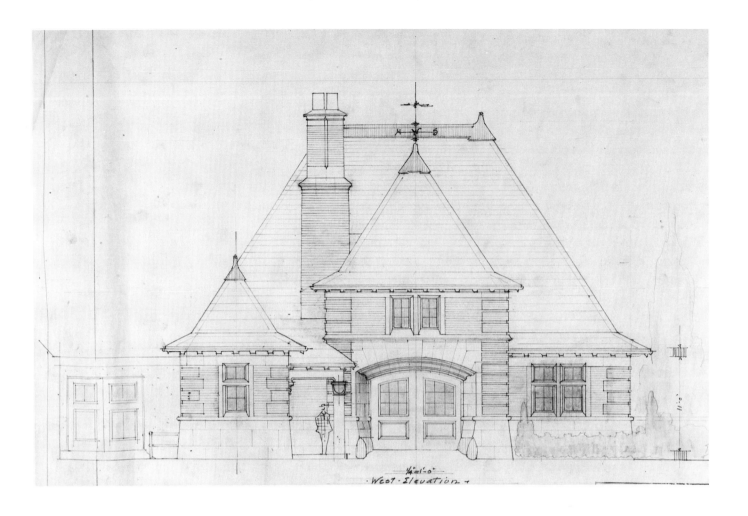

Lyman H. Treadway garage, 1918.

One of the most interesting structures is the garage for Lyman H. Treadway built in 1918 behind the Euclid Avenue house that Dyer's firm designed for him in 1910. Treadway was a member of the first board of directors of the Fourth Federal Reserve District, which undoubtedly stood Walker and Weeks in good stead later when its new building was planned. The house, now obscured by the Health Museum of Cleveland, is a sort of cross between the informal and the revivalist tendencies, with the symmetrical front and dormers of colonial revival house and the spreading hip roof of a more modern one. The garage (no longer called a carriage house) is as large as many residences, with room for five automobiles (the place for each car was marked on the plans), workroom, storeroom, tool room, potting room, greenhouse, and the chauffeur's room. The dominant element is a steep, fanciful hip roof whose elegant curve at the eaves

Edward G. Buckwell residence, Cleveland Heights, 1915.

has an Oriental suggestion. The heavily quoined brick and stucco walls are subordinated to the main roof and a multiplicity of smaller roofs on wings and dormers, creating a picturesque effect that is thoroughly late Victorian. But it is noteworthy that the imposing result is made by contrasting shapes, volumes, and materials, not ornamentation.

A house in which the outsized sheltering roof reached its culmination was designed for Walter S. Bowler in 1915. Bowler was a vice president of the Lake Shore Banking and Trust Company, for which Walker and Weeks did an important building alteration in 1919. Standing on South Park Boulevard in Shaker Heights, the house is sheathed with shingles and presents a broad front to the street, which is the long arm of an L-shaped plan. The great roof with four dormers slopes down to the left end of the facade to extend over a small side porch supported by short round columns.

The irregularity of the Treadway and Bowler facades dramatically emphasizes the differences in the more revivalist houses. An elegant example of the latter was designed for Edward G. Buckwell, secretary of the Cleveland Twist Drill Company, in 1915. The Buckwell house, interestingly, addresses its narrow end to Chestnut Hills Drive in Cleveland Heights. There is a fully developed facade on each of the two side elevations, although the garden front, because of the way the street curves at that point,

Charles L. Murfey residence, Shaker
Heights, 1916.

can also be seen by the passerby. The design sources are from the English
Georgian period. The end elevation has three windows topped with semi-
circular terra-cotta lunettes. The main entrance front has a pillared stoop
with a Palladian window above, and the garden elevation is also centered
on a Venetian motif consisting of three sets of tripartite windows. The
interior plan is a variation on the informal center-hall type that was already well established.

Walker and Weeks's purest colonial revival house was built for Charles
L. Murfey on South Park Boulevard in Shaker Heights in 1917. Murfey
was a vice president of the Guardian Savings and Trust Company, for
which Walker and Weeks designed one of their first major bank buildings
in 1915. Placing the house on a vast front lawn, the architects looked to
the Virginia manner of the Georgian type. The facade is clearly based on
plantation houses like Carter's Grove and Westover. In order to accommodate the development of the freer interior plan of the suburban house,
the two flanking offices of the original prototype were connected to the
main block. Thus, one becomes the typical sun porch beyond the living
room and the other the kitchen wing. The rest of the interior plan is a
subtle compromise between twentieth-century informality and Georgian
symmetry.

Much of this residential work, both in the suburbs and the country,
went on during the First World War. More than a year after the United
States entered in war in April 1917, the federal government appropriated

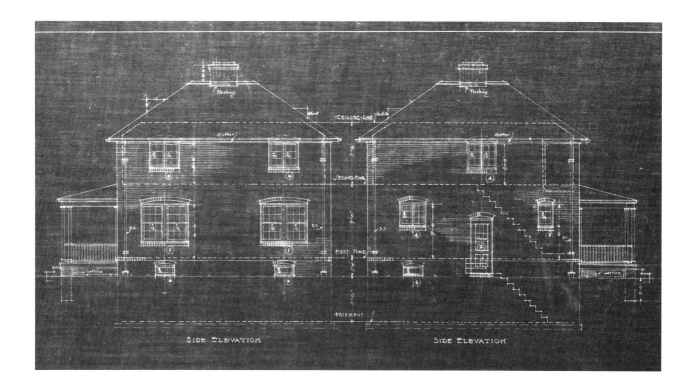

One of several designs for Alliance Houses, Alliance, 1918.

money to build housing for workers in war factories and munitions plants. In May 1918 several cities in Ohio were chosen as locations for the housing assistance; among them was Alliance, an industrial town of eighteen thousand located about sixty-five miles southeast of Cleveland. Alliance was the home of Morgan Engineering, manufacturer of the first electric overhead traveling cranes, which was then devoting its entire production to gun mounts for the U.S. Army Ordnance. Company president William H. Morgan was the local contact with the Bureau of Industrial Housing and Transportation of the Department of Labor. One million dollars was allotted for the Alliance housing, and the project was awarded to Walker and Weeks.[13]

The plans, ready for the local contractors in August 1918, called for 181 houses, of which eighty-nine were actually built. Several different types were proposed for the five-, six-, and seven-room houses, all constructed of brick. They were of three basic forms: a simple rectangular style with a gable roof parallel to the street; a square style with a pyramidal roof; and a similar style with a hip roof that slanted down over the porch, bungalow-fashion. All had the most current central heating, plumbing, and electrical systems and a single central chimney. The simple, straightforward design gave them a progressive look for the period. They were, in fact, greatly scaled-down versions of the Judd and Renkert houses of 1912–14.

S. Prentiss Baldwin residence, 1920.

In spite of the sudden and dramatic collapse of Germany in November 1918, the Alliance housing project was completed and ready for occupancy in May 1919. The government rented the houses for a year and then sold them to the public in 1920. This "government addition" neighborhood of several square blocks was still fully occupied and well maintained seventy years later, testifying to the excellent design and construction of the original concept.

In the twenties Walker and Weeks designed far fewer residences than in the previous decade, but those they did design display the high tide of revivalism to the best advantage and demonstrate beyond question that the successful architect with a wide-ranging practice did not ordinarily have a single identifiable style. They also reveal that, beyond using the standard and accepted historical revival sources of the academic school, the architects of the twenties extended the range of those sources. Four of those Walker and Weeks houses are worth particular mention.

In the Wade Park allotment at University Circle, the firm in 1921 designed and planned the last of the large mansions to be erected there. Built for S. Prentiss Baldwin, with whom Frank Walker was working so closely on the revival of Gates Mills, the house stood on East Boulevard on the present site of the Cleveland Institute of Music. It was a fitting neighbor to Mrs. John Hay's house by Abram Garfield across the street and a logical successor to Walker and Weeks's mansion for Benedict Crowell two blocks away. Also a Renaissance villa, the Baldwin house had a symmetrical facade and a hip roof, an arched entrance with a columned porte-cochere, and a servants' wing. Inside, a grand hall opened

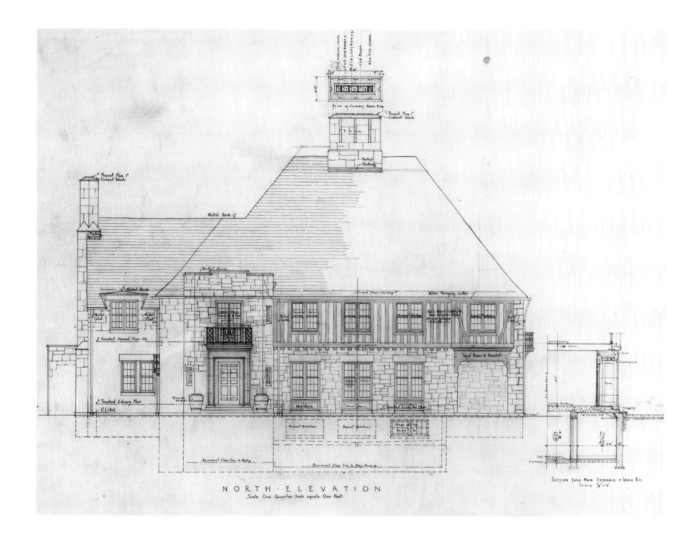

N O R T H · E L E V A T I O N
Scale One Quarter Inch equals One Foot.

Armen H. Tashjian residence, Cleveland Heights, 1923.

into a living room measuring twenty by forty feet, and upstairs were eight bedrooms for the family and four for the servants. The Renaissance detail of Tuscan pilasters, window surrounds, and balustrades was scholarly and correct.

A noteworthy eclectic design was built in 1924 for Walker and Weeks's engineer, Armen H. Tashjian, on Fairmount Boulevard in Cleveland Heights. It is distinguished by an enormous hipped roof, fully as tall as the two stories of the house below, with a great center chimney at the ridge. No doubt because of this roof, McAlester places the Tashjian house in the French eclectic pigeonhole.[14] The house has the basic shape of the simple wartime industrial housing in Alliance. However, the form is elaborated with a projecting entrance tower, a random ashlar stone first story, and a half-timbered second story, making a highly individual statement. (The drawings for the house are initialed "J.B.H.," which was certainly J. Byers Hays.)

The range of revivalist sources is further illuminated by the house designed in 1929 for Henry A. Taylor, U.S. Postmaster in Cleveland, and erected in Cleveland Heights. For this house the architects went to the indigenous Connecticut Western Reserve farmhouses of northeastern Ohio, or the early-nineteenth-century Greek revival. The characteristic form is a two-and-a-half-story gable-end facade with a wing extending to one side. The Taylor house is fairly pedestrian and not too convincing historically, since the first story is of stone veneer and the second story of clapboard siding. A sloping site to the rear of the lot adds some interest to the house, but its chief importance is the evidence that revivalist sources were not limited to the accepted European or academic styles.

A final residential scheme planned in 1928 was never executed, but it nevertheless deserves mention because it was such an extraordinary fantasy to come from Walker and Weeks's drawing boards. It was designed for William H. Hunt, for whom Walker and Weeks had done alterations on an older house in 1916 and garden plans in 1924. Hunt, an executive in the building brick and insurance businesses, was a pillar of the conservative establishment, a board member of the Hiram House settlement, chairman of the Chamber of Commerce City Plan Commission for six years, and philanthropist—all of which make the oddity of the design all the more remarkable. Here, to all appearances, was an extensive shingle-style mansion from the 1880s, embellished with a stone porte-cochere having wide pointed arches and, sprouting from the rooftop, two octagonal turrets with peaked roofs, one twenty feet in diameter and the other perhaps half that size. Maybe the eccentric design was never intended to be built as drawn, or perhaps the project was overtaken by the Great Depression. The plans for the estate in Independence south of Cleveland also show a series of terraced promenades stepping down the flanks of the Cuyahoga River Valley, and these in fact were constructed and still exist today.

It is a pretty safe presumption that Frank Walker himself enjoyed designing residences above all. Most of the challenges involved in a large building are present in the smaller project but on a scale that can be managed by an individual designer. Likewise, only one client needs to be satisfied, as compared to a board, a committee, or a set of departments. On the few occasions when Walker and Weeks were awarded something big enough to be called a mansion, they acquitted themselves with excellent marks, but they devoted just as much thought and care to the more modest commission. Walker's lifelong commitment to the development of Gates Mills was really a special chapter in the personal career of a man who was a part of the social circle of its inhabitants. The involvement of an architect like Walker in the re-creation of the village was one of the last phases of nineteenth-century historical revivalism.

On the other hand, Walker and Weeks's public housing revealed a concern for humane living conditions for everyone, reflecting their education, training, and early practice, which took place in a period of social reform. The progressive idea was manifested in the detached houses on individual lots (as contrasted with the tenements, apartments, or row houses of other private and public multiple housing), in the simple but sensible floor plans, and in the use of permanent but economical materials. While the worker's house was not as grand as the manufacturer's residence, the two were based on similar principles.

Walker and Weeks are not known for creating new forms or styles; they belonged to that fortunate generation of residential architects who reached a consensus on the nature of "gracious living." The question of style does not seem to have been a terribly critical one. Walker and Weeks were designing for upper-middle-class and well-to-do clients who wanted comfort, good materials and craftsmanship, and a reasonable economy. The presence or absence of a strong high-style statement, while not entirely inconsequential, was apparently not foremost in the minds of Walker and Weeks's domestic clients. In moving easily from the generalized eclecticism of the early twentieth century to the more archaeologically correct revivals, the architects were riding the wave of current fashion rather than leading it; and whereas the period revivalism of the twenties permitted a broad range of choices, it was obvious that Walker himself felt much more at home with the neoclassical and American colonial idioms. The firm's few designs in the other chief alternative, the Tudor revival, were done by other designers in the firm. As it turned out, however, Walker and Weeks become known not for their residences but for their banking, public, commercial, and institutional buildings.

chapter 3

BANK ARCHITECTS

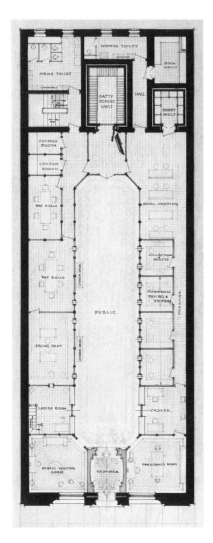

One of several designs for the National City Bank, Akron, 1912.

A SMALL CLASSICAL building designed in 1912 for National City Bank in Akron was important neither for its size nor especially for its style. Rather, it was the first in the series of banks that became Walker and Weeks's principal work for several years and eventually resulted in more than a hundred buildings in seven states. The facade of the Akron bank was a simple restatement of the design for the First National Bank in Cleveland that was done by Dyer's office in 1904–6; the original design for which Walker and Weeks were likely responsible. The square front of four Corinthian columns (or two columns and two pilasters), the large intercolumnar windows, and the balustrade on the parapet were identical in the two banks, as were other details.

In the teens nearly three dozen bank projects came into the Walker and Weeks office, almost surpassing the number of residences in the same period. Both the general conditions in the country and the firm's business practices account for this large number. Pivotal was the passage of the Federal Reserve Act in December 1913; the creation of a central banking system did much to overcome defects in the existing national bank system. The relationship of a Federal Reserve Bank to its member banks was similar to that of a commercial bank to its customers. The establishment of greater money reserves for the member banks and control of the currency created a more stable environment in which the thousands of existing banks could flourish. The country was divided into twelve Federal Reserve Districts, and when Cleveland was designated as the headquarters of the Fourth District, the city became the financial center for one of the richest industrial and manufacturing regions in the country, with more than seven hundred national banks located in the district.

Moreover, the total money supply increased drastically during the First World War. Because the financing of the war was only partially paid for by taxes, the U.S. Treasury had to be funded largely through the sale of government bonds. There was little serious effort to discourage the creation of money, and with the addition of ineffective or nonexistent price controls, one of the results was considerable inflation. The situation

Guardian Savings and Trust
Building, 1915, interior stairway.

Guardian Savings and Trust Building, 1915, entrance.

created an environment that was favorable to the growth of banks, especially in an expanding region like northeastern Ohio.

Of the early Cleveland banks by Walker and Weeks, only a handful were remodelings of existing quarters in nineteenth-century buildings; the great majority were new buildings. The largest and most ambitious remodeling, if such a major undertaking can be called that, was the transformation of the New England Building into the Guardian Savings and

Trust Building (National City Bank) in 1915. The original building was designed by Shepley, Rutan & Coolidge of Boston (the successor firm of Henry H. Richardson) and erected in 1896. The biography of Charles A. Coolidge included the New England Building among the firm's "most important buildings";[15] the sandstone-faced structure was an elegant example of a tall office building with restrained Renaissance detail. The original tower on Euclid Avenue had only the depth of one double-loaded corridor. Walker and Weeks designed a seventeen-story addition extending the building through the block to Vincent Street, making it among the most ambitious tall buildings they had done to date.

The principal changes to the original building were the alteration of the lower facade and the addition of a grand new banking room. The round-arched portal of the New England Building was replaced by a colonnade of four colossal three-story Corinthian columns (which were built around the existing structural steel columns). The facade does not truly harmonize with the upper stories by Shepley, Rutan & Coolidge, but the street scale is so large that the discrepancy is seldom noted. It is a curious commentary that the temporary wooden structure erected over the sidewalk to protect pedestrians resulted in a round-arched arcade that complemented the original New England Building better than the new facade.

In order to judge the final appearance of the proposed interior design, Walker and Weeks had a completely detailed scale model made by the premier architectural sculptors and model makers in Cleveland, Fischer and Jirouch. The new bank entrance leads into a majestic room on the basilica plan with two rows of Corinthian columns and a flat coffered ceiling. The walls, columns, counters, and customers' desks are of pink Georgia marble, the ceiling is richly painted, and the bronze work is finished in gold. It seems likely that the result was instrumental in enhancing Walker and Weeks's already-established reputation in bank design.

The combination bank and office building was a distinct type in the prewar period that found expression in many new buildings. Their designs, from ten to twenty stories tall, followed a common pattern. A classical street facade of two or three stories proved a base for a shaft of identical floors, which in turn was topped by a separate band of upper stories, a colonnaded section, or simply a cornice. Almost without exception these buildings were faced with stone, Indiana limestone, sometimes marble or granite for the street-level stories, terra-cotta ornamentation, or, on occasion, a matte, glazed brick for the main shaft. The interior banking room was usually a single long, rectangular space and frequently had an elevated platform for the bank officers at one end. Or it might have columned aisles, like the Guardian Bank, a flat-beamed or coffered ceiling, a shallow vaulted ceiling, or, rarely, an open truss roof. Access to the office

Lorain County Savings and Trust Building, Elyria, 1916.

tower was provided by a separate elevator lobby located either at the main entrance before entering the banking room or through a different entrance at the side or rear of the building.

This formula had two principal stylistic variations. The street facade might have two or more neoclassic columns or pilasters, and these could be in any of the major classical orders. One of the best examples of this type is the Lorain County Savings and Trust building in Elyria, designed in 1916. The eleven-story building has four Tuscan columns on the facade, an elevator lobby just beyond the entrance vestibule, and a banking room illuminated by a skylight. In the second variation, the street facade was a round-arched Renaissance arcade, with the masonry joints of the

Steubenville Bank and Trust Building,
Steubenville, 1919.

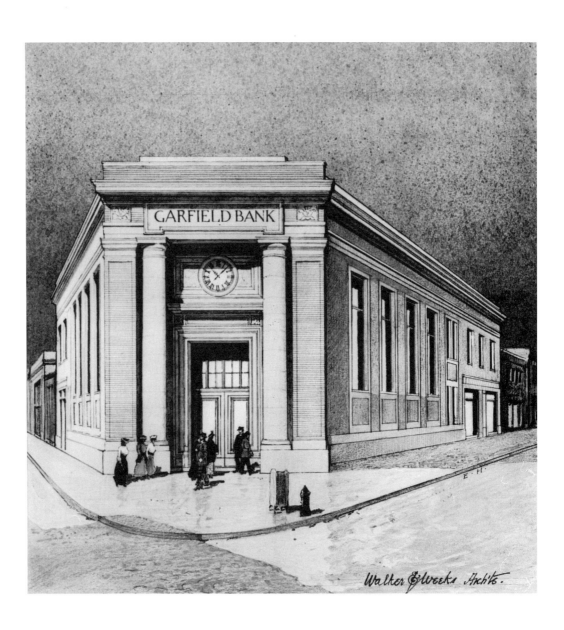

Garfield Savings Bank, St. Clair Avenue at East 79th Street, 1915.

stonework usually emphasized in the Florentine manner. One of the finest examples is the Steubenville Savings and Trust building, planned in 1919, with its eleven-story tower with seven imposing arches on the long street elevation.

Of the many smaller banks, one of the more striking buildings was designed for the expanding Garfield Savings Bank in Cleveland, for which Walker and Weeks planned two branches in 1915. The building on St. Clair Avenue at East 79th Street stands at the triangular intersection of three streets and forms an irregular quadrilateral with the entrance at the narrow end, framed by two Tuscan columns. Like many bank buildings

First National Bank of Cleveland, 1917.

of the period, it incorporated space on two stories for rental as retail stores. But unlike most, it is built of brick rather than stone. The Garfield Bank is also illustrative of the consolidation and mergers that typified the twenties. The bank merged with the Cleveland Trust Company in 1922, and the next year its president, Harris Creech, became president of Cleveland Trust. So the Garfield Bank became part of the phenomenal expansion of Cleveland Trust, which eventually operated more than fifty branches in the city of Cleveland.

One of the greatest mergers in the financial history of Cleveland aborted several bank buildings already being planned by Walker and Weeks. On December 31, 1920, the Union Trust Company was formed by the merger of three major banks and twenty-six other financial institutions. Among the companies were five for which Walker and Weeks had plans under way. They were working on additions or alterations to their own Union National Bank building and Dyer's First National Bank and had designed, and had final working drawings for, major new buildings for Citizens Savings and Trust, Broadway Savings and Trust, and Woodland Avenue Savings and Trust.

Some of the unbuilt projects are as interesting as many that were actually executed. For the plan to enlarge the First National Bank at 241 Euclid Avenue, which contemplated extending it through to Superior Avenue, a voluminous number of sketches were made. The most elaborate scheme extended the length of the old banking room through the block; a rotunda at the north end compensated for the awkward change in the angle of Euclid and Superior Avenues, and a regal circular staircase descended to the lower level of Superior. However, the key interest of the plan lies in the fact that the Superior Avenue facade was a tall square tower on the axis of the mall based on Daniel Burnham's 1903 Group Plan. (A vertical accent at the south end of the Mall was envisioned by many planners over the years but not fully realized until the completion of the Sohio [BP America] Building in 1985.) Walker and Weeks's tower was freely based on campaniles like those of San Marco in Venice or the Giralda in Seville, which also was the inspiration for the Terminal Tower less than ten years later.

By 1920 Walker and Weeks occasionally listed themselves in city directories as "Bank Architects and Engineers." Over the next decade, they planned at least twenty banks in Cleveland, twice as many in the rest of Ohio, and more than twenty in other states. During the first half of the twenties, most banks were still designed in the classical styles, either neoclassic or Renaissance, in the manner that had been fixed in the teens. Walker and Weeks designed especially notable buildings in Cleveland, Toledo, Youngstown, Canton, and Massillon, Ohio. The Federal Reserve

THE FEDERAL RESERVE BANK OF CLEVELAND

Federal Reserve Bank of Cleveland, 1921,
proposed design.

Federal Reserve Bank of Cleveland, 1921.

Bank of Cincinnati was located in the fourteen-story Chamber of Commerce building, and Walker and Weeks were associated with its architects, Tietig & Lee and Hake & Kuck of Cincinnati. They even planned a thirty-eight-story office building in New York City for the Harriman Bank on Fifth Avenue and 44th Street. Although the building was eventually erected from plans by New York architect H. Craig Severance, it bears an indisputable resemblance to Walker and Weeks's proposed design. Its shape, a tall central tower rising from a series of receding blocks, was determined by the New York zoning laws and represented serious compromises between economic demands and the classical formula.

Federal Reserve Bank of Cleveland, 1921, interior.

The undisputed crown in the array of more than a hundred banks during Walker and Weeks's career was the Federal Reserve Bank of Cleveland. The Fourth District Federal Reserve Bank opened in the Williamson Building on Public Square in 1914, but it was not until 1919 that planning began for a new building. In November of that year, the architects began their conferences with officials of the bank to develop the building program, and in April 1920 they began the conceptual development of the plan. Since the building would be free-standing with daylight on all four sides, the elevators, mechanical ducts and conduits, toilets, and employee's lockers were placed in a central core. The main public lobby and banking room were on the 6th Street side of the first floor, whose complex plan accommodated a great many different ingeniously arranged functions. The offices for the governor, the chairman, and other executives, plus conference rooms, reception rooms, a dining room, and library, were on the eighth floor. The tenth floor was the personnel floor, with a cafeteria, a gymnasium, and recreation and reading rooms. The number of typical working floors needed between the upper and lower floors determined the height of the building. The bank's vaults required special attention, and in 1920 and 1921 tests were made to experiment with the construction and demolition of various types of walls. The York vault door, the largest ever built, was forty-eight inches thick. It took nearly a year to complete the working drawings, and construction began in 1922. The general contractor was John Gill & Sons, a Cleveland builder whose credentials included major public buildings in Washington, D.C., Baltimore, New Jersey, and Missouri (and soon Cleveland's Terminal Tower).

The design of the Federal Reserve Bank building, like that of the major public buildings on the nearby Mall, evokes the ideals of the early-twentieth-century American Renaissance. The adaptation of classic architectural styles, the symbolic representation of ideas, and the principle of collaboration between architects and decorative artists were the earmarks of that ideal. The impact of the Federal Reserve Bank depended on the combination of lavish materials, superlative craftsmanship (the best sculptors and artists were employed to ornament the building), and the ornamental scheme.

The style is based on the fortress palaces of the merchant princes of fifteenth-century Florence and Rome. The building is classically proportioned, 200 feet long on East 6th Street and 150 feet on Superior Avenue and is 200 feet tall (the square and the ratio of three to four); most of the other dimensions can also be expressed in simple ratios of whole numbers, as in the teachings of Vitruvius, Alberti, and Palladio. This foursquare structure stands on a base of pink granite, and the upper stories are clad in a pinkish Georgia marble with textures that are more rugged at the base and graduated toward the top of the building. Arguably, no other architects of the time could have surpassed the taste and skill with which the majestic rusticated arcade of the lower story is detailed. On either side of the main entrance stand the draped allegorical figures of Integrity and Security (sculptured by Henry Hering of New York) posed in the familiar attitude of Liberty. Above the entrance, the metopes of the entablature represent ancient coins, referring to the origins of modern currency. The Superior Avenue entrance to the office building is guarded by an overlifesized bronze figure of Energy seated on a broken pediment, also sculptured by Hering. A rusticated niche forms a backdrop for the statue; the same niche is repeated at

Cleveland Discount Building, 1921.

the opposite Rockwell Street entrance to the truck courtyard, where the sculpture is replaced by a barred guard post.

The interior of the public lobby is a high groin-vaulted hall with deeply coffered and gilded ceilings and a low dome on pendentives at the intersection of the transverse and axial halls. The walls are faced with a rich, gold-veined Siena marble, and each arched bay is screened by high, black wrought-iron screens. One observer has likened the experience of entering the bank to walking into the inside of a bar of gold. The fortress image, the proportions, the allegorical sculpture, and the expressive materials and fine craftsmanship combined to realize the Renaissance ideal. The functional yet symbolic design of the Federal Reserve Bank, and its happy relationship to the buildings on the mall, make it one of Walker and Weeks's major accomplishments.

Just half a block east of the Federal Reserve Bank is one of the most characteristic buildings of the twenties in another sense, as the story of the building exemplifies the speculative mania of the decade. Josiah Kirby was a Cleveland businessman who formed the Cleveland Discount Company as a giant mortgage corporation dealing in large construction loans. When Kirby began the Cleveland Discount Building (subsequently the Guarantee Title Building, then the NBC Building, and finally the Superior Building) in 1921, the company's capital was listed at $37 million. The company went into receivership in February 1923, however, its stock worthless, and the assets were sold. Later Kirby had a succession of other business failures and was finally indicted by a federal grand jury for fraud and stock manipulation.

The Cleveland Discount Building forms the terminus of a procession of five buildings along Superior Avenue from Public Square that has been called one of the most remarkable classical ensembles in America. Three of them are by Walker and Weeks—the Public Library, the Federal Reserve Bank, and the Cleveland Discount Building. In its own fashion the latter is almost as lavishly detailed as the Federal Reserve. The base and monumental Doric order of the facade are of gray granite, the upper stories are of gray glazed brick, and the cornices and friezes are of exquisitely detailed matching terra-cotta. Behind the entrance columns is a finely wrought metalwork grill. The lobby, banking room, and office corridors were sheathed from floor to ceiling in marble and mosaic. One might say that the fate of Kirby is symbolized by that of the main banking room, which was later partitioned and destroyed. But his building stands as a reminder of one of the more colorful, but less savory, aspects of the Roaring Twenties.

In the mid-twenties a dramatic new approach to the style of the bank office building made its appearance. With the design of the Old National

Old National City Bank Building, Lima, 1925.

City Bank in Lima, Ohio, in 1925, Walker and Weeks were in the vanguard of a new style. The problem of the tall office building had been sharply focused in the 1922 competition for the *Chicago Tribune* Building. The second-place design, by Eliel Saarinen, was recognized by many as a far more logical and powerful expression of the height, structure, and function of the tall office building than the winning Gothic design. The characteristic vertical lines and setback masses soon influenced many other buildings. By 1925, these features appeared in a number of telephone buildings across the country, perhaps because they housed a modern, developing technology. The Pacific Telephone and Telegraph Building in San Francisco was already completed, and the frequently admired New York Telephone Building by McKenzie, Voorhees and Gmelin was being planned, as well as Hubbell and Benes's Ohio Bell Telephone Building in Cleveland. On all of these, the distinctive features were the emphasis on the vertical piers and recessed window spandrels, the projection of the piers above the roof line, the setback masses of the upper stories, and the simplification or complete abandonment of traditional ornament.

It is thus all the more unusual that the style was found in a bank building in a city of forty-two thousand in western Ohio. The Lima bank was designed by October 1925 and completed in 1927. The building is a slender fourteen-story shaft only five bays wide on the front, and the side elevations, which are twice as long, are completely finished architecturally. There is a single setback at the topmost floor, and the total effect is like a miniature sketch for Rockefeller Center's RCA Building six years later. The ornamental window spandrels were of lead instead of the aluminum universally used within a few years. The banking room has round-arched windows and a shallow coved ceiling, but the lines are completely simple and geometric with none of the coffered and gilded historical detail of the earlier banks.

Walker and Weeks worked variations on the style in two more banking towers erected in 1929–30, the Central Savings and Trust in Akron and the Lincoln National Bank of Fort Wayne, Indiana. Like architects everywhere, they were experimenting with different solutions to the crown of the modern office tower, a design challenge whose most spectacular resolution was achieved on the Chrysler Building in New York. The Lincoln National Bank rises as a square tower for sixteen of its twenty-two floors, then diminishes in three stages to end in an octagonal story. Finally it is topped by a cupola not unlike a small version of the Empire State Building's mooring mast. Different spandrels were used on different parts of the facade, some of stone, some of metal, and some of terra-cotta. The richness of the ornament is breathtaking, and the geometric floral designs are of the kind that would now be called pure art deco motifs.

One of several designs for the Central Savings and Trust Building, Akron, 1929.

The twenty-seven-story Akron bank is a square tower with setbacks at the fourteenth, twentieth, and twenty-fifth stories, though the diagonal corner elements of the topmost stage made a somewhat awkward transition from the main tower. The piers of the three lower floors are fluted shafts framing ornamental cartouches, the stamp of the whole also being nonhistorical in character. Walker and Weeks did not have a style name for the massing and ornament of these buildings, but they did call the Central Savings and Trust "modern."

This bank and office building is an expression of architecture in its modern phase, not the extreme manifestation of modern art, but a rational expression intended as a contribution to the trend of the times in the working out of an office building. . . .

The Architectural profession has made tremendous strides in the last decade in overcoming the old practice of evasion and deception concerning uses of space and materials by the present-day solution in the skyscraper. The custom of employing old architectural forms which no longer serve functions has been supplanted by the adaption of new forms that follow the required efficiency in the functions of today.[16]

As bank architects, Walker and Weeks carved out a niche for themselves; for more than a decade they had no peers within three hundred miles of Cleveland. The reasons seem to be found in the combination of aggressive salesmanship, competent delivery of services, and superior design. The cities and towns of the Midwest are full of familiar classical banks built in the teens and twenties, when the economic climate and the growth of the cities created an almost unprecedented environment for building. What is notable is that Walker and Weeks brought a surprising variety to the genre, in spite of the fact that the fundamental program of many banks was very similar. An unusual site, size, or complexity and the combination of a bank with offices, stores, a hotel, or apartments offered a variety of challenges to be met. In stylistic terms, one wonders whether academic architects would ever have come to the end of the possibilities of the neoclassical and Renaissance idioms. But the temple front, the colonnade, the arch, and the rusticated wall were manipulated by Walker and Weeks in ways that produced more than a hundred permutations. This versatility resulted in everything from the marble and granite monument of the Federal Reserve system in Cleveland to the one-room small-town bank, from the home for a small family operation to the one for a speculative manipulator.

In the application of the modernistic idiom on the Old National City Bank of Lima in 1925, Walker and Weeks were precocious. Their adoption of the idiom on the heels of the *Chicago Tribune* competition antedated all but a few exercises elsewhere in the country. The new building massing and stylized geometric ornament opened up a whole new range of possibilities. It is interesting to speculate where the development of the style might have gone if it had not been for the onset of the Great Depression and the arrival of the European international style. Walker was among several of his contemporaries who saw the modernistic development as the harbinger of a new, indigenous "American style." Before it was overtaken by the international modern style, it succeeded in producing many spectacular examples of commercial and public buildings.

chapter 4

COMMERCIAL BUILDINGS

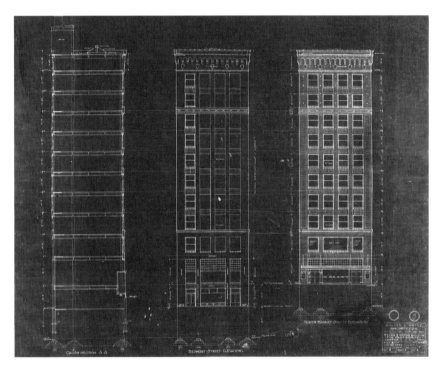

Renkert Building, Canton, 1912.

THE COMMERCIAL architecture of Walker and Weeks reveals the same versatility—or ambivalence, depending on one's point of view—as their residences and banks. Probably fashion and the whims of clients were equally responsible. The business clients of the early teens were members of the nineteenth-century breed of personal proprietors. The head of a company was a man who started with an idea and some capital, and businesses were run by their owners; the late-twentieth-century corporate boards that spread the decision-making responsibility would have been utterly alien to them. Thus, for example, the construction of the Renkert Building in Canton, Ohio, by Harry S. Renkert of the Metropolitan Paving Brick Company, was described as a "personal venture."[17] Harry was the brother of Oliver Renkert, later president of the company, whose home Walker and Weeks designed two years later. Planned and erected in 1912–13, the Renkert Building was called "the first skyscraper office building in Stark County."[18] Fifteen- and twenty-story buildings had been erected in Cleveland by 1900, but in a city of fifty thousand a ten-story building was still a wonder.

A long, narrow block whose main street facade is only one-fourth as wide as the long elevation on the side street, the Renkert Building is a nearly perfect demonstration of Louis Sullivan's idea of a tall office building. The vertical piers are emphasized and the horizontal spandrels slightly recessed, the lower stories are devoid of ornamentation, and the only

Bingham Company Warehouse, 1915
(Martin Linsey).

concession to contemporary taste is the handsome but restrained arcaded corbeling at the cornice. The design clearly expresses its steel frame construction. The technology of the steel skeleton was well understood and widely disseminated by the beginning of the century, and this building reveals the mastery of its architectural expression by Walker and Weeks. The Renkert company's paving brick provides the facing of the outer walls of the frame, makes a durable curtain wall, and gives the building a beautiful orange-red color.

A great warehouse erected in 1914–15 for a pioneer Cleveland hardware firm, the Bingham Company was claimed to be the largest single unit for wholesale hardware merchandising in the world. The block-long, L-shaped structure is especially interesting because of the steep difference in the grade level between the front and the back of the block. The eight-story building has a sophisticated exterior design related to that of

Goodyear Tire and Rubber Company
Building, Akron, 1917, detail.

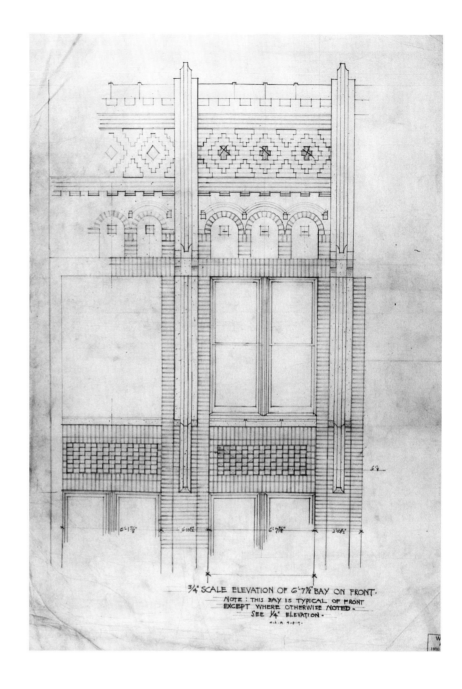

the Renkert Building, with simple repetitive piers giving architectural expression to the steel and concrete structure. It also faced with brick, and the roof line consists of an utterly plain concave cornice reminiscent of Root's Monadnock Building. The subtle refinements of detail and proportion raise the architecture of the Bingham building above that of its neighbors in the warehouse district, and its design "demonstrates the difference between building and architecture."[19]

Only a few other modest exercises for industrial clients marked Walker and Weeks's first decade. Brick detailing gave some architectural distinction to the generally utilitarian shell of steel column construction of an American Express Company garage built on Lakeside Avenue in Cleveland in 1917.

A special opportunity came when the Goodyear Tire and Rubber Company in Akron decided to erect a large employees' recreation building, Goodyear Hall, in 1917. The progressive management was headed by P. W. Litchfield, who stated that the building was "a monument to the fact that hereafter, Goodyear intends to devote its energies to the building of men instead of the building of the machine."[20] This kind of benevolent paternalism is one of the most misunderstood and least appreciated phenomena in the history of the early-twentieth-century industrial entrepreneurs. Also at the time Goodyear initiated an "Industrial Assembly," a radical experiment in employee self-government that operated successfully for sixteen years.

Walker and Weeks's Goodyear Hall, a six-story, block-long brick-faced structure, harmonized with the original factory across the street. The upper story and parapet were articulated by diaper-pattern and arcaded brick and by vertical turretlike piers whose lines would later be called art deco. The ground floor on Market Street contained retail shops. The clubhouse contained the largest gymnasium in Ohio (during the First World War it was used for balloon assembly), classrooms, a library, laboratories, club meeting rooms, bowling alleys, billiard rooms, a rifle range, and a cafeteria with its own bakery. The fourth floor was reserved for women and contained a community room, lockers and showers, domestic science rooms, and social and recreational activity rooms. The grace and elegance of the auditorium were consistent with the idea of employee improvement. A theater seating 1,786 was the last unit of the building to be completed, opening in April 1920.

At the triangular corner formed by East Market Street and Goodyear Boulevard, the company also erected a bank building that connected to the hall. Until 1933 it was occupied by the Ohio Savings and Trust Company, of which F. A. Seiberling was the president; then the building became the Goodyear Bank, at the time the only company-owned bank in Ohio. In contrast to the hall, it is a thoroughly Renaissance design, with five arched windows on each of the converging elevations and rusticated banded columns in the sixteenth-century Italian mannerist style at the entrance.

Unlike the industrial work, but like the banks and office buildings, the architecture of retail commerce tended to be conservative and classical. In Cleveland, just before the eve of the First World War, the Euclid Avenue business district between East 9th Street and Playhouse Square was rapidly being built up. The Statler Hotel, Union Club, Cleveland Athletic Club, Sterling and Welch, and Halle's and Higbee's department stores were all established around East 12th Street. The most interesting challenge for the retail developer was what to do with the empty John Hartness Brown Building just east of East 9th Street. The six-story building, with four acres of floor space, was an experimental all-glass art nouveau building designed by Warren and Wetmore, architects of New Yorks's Grand Central Station.[21] Because of the owner's financial reverses, and because no one believed in 1901 that the retail district would move beyond East 9th Street, it stood unfinished and vacant for a dozen years. In 1912–13 the B. R. Baker Store employed Walker and Weeks to renovate the western third of the building (1001 Euclid), and the Loomis Company had them remodel the eastern third (1021 Euclid); and in 1915 George B. Post & Sons were engaged to design the new front for the remaining section. In the renovations, however, the remarkable original glass wall was covered with classical facades. Yet in the opinion of the 1914 reviewer, the Loomis building, then occupied by Stearn and Company, "shows a delicious treatment of terra cotta in its lighter forms. The charming play of light and shade in the cornice with its bold yet delicate corbels, the decorative forms of the panels and the marquise with its air of confidence combine to make a building both chaste and dignified."[22] Immediately to the east was the Stillman Building which Walker and Weeks designed in 1913 and which housed Siegel's store and later the entrance to the Stillman Theater. Its facade "is cast in a different mold. The element of decoration enters more strongly than in the earlier structure, but the decoration is applied to strengthen the feeling of solid construction and to give the building by contrast with its neighbor a distinction of its own."[23]

With the opening of the Stillman Theater in 1916, developer Joseph Laronge envisioned the fashionable strip of fine shops, restaurants, and theaters between East 9th and East 17th Streets that became Playhouse Square. At East 14th Street, Walker and Weeks executed the first of the future Playhouse Square buildings in 1912. The Kinney and Levan store, which claimed to be one of the largest exclusive home furnishings stores in the nation, was sandwiched between the Selzer Building, where the Bulkley Building and Allen Theater would be built in 1921, and the future

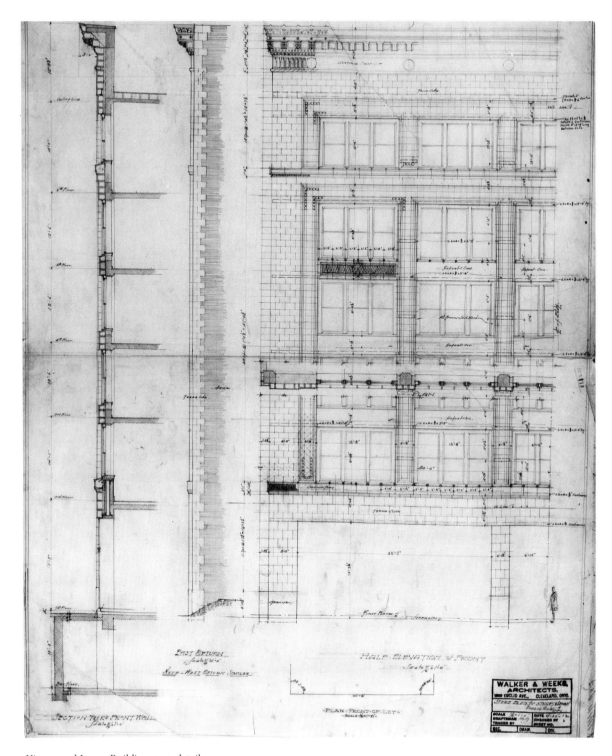

Kinney and Levan Building, 1912, detail.

site of the Lindner Building. Its six-story, nearly square classical facade (now the Playhouse Square Building) set the standard for all the buildings that would follow in the district in the early 1920s. Moreover, the architects furnished the interiors of these retails specialty stores with elegant architectural details in the late art nouveau or the new art deco styles.

Throughout the teens and twenties Walker and Weeks continued to make their mark on Cleveland's downtown. As always, some projects were new buildings, some additions or renovations, and some remained unbuilt. They designed the simple but gracious Cowell and Hubbard building on Euclid at East 13th Street in 1919–20. They supervised alterations to the storefronts of the Arcade and the interior of the Caxton Building. For Wolfe's Music Store in the 2100 block of Euclid Avenue they made a little three-story building of gemlike craftsmanship in snow-white terra-cotta, marble, and bronze.

By the midtwenties, Walker and Weeks's reputation brought them commissions in dozens of Ohio cities and in eleven states. Apart from the banks and office buildings, their Ohio work included a clinic/hospital for the internationally important Lima Locomotive Works. They worked on the Coca-Cola headquarters in Atlanta and designed a proposed office building for the Southern Railway in Washington, D.C. An office building in Frank Walker's hometown of Pittsfield took them back to Massachusetts. For Cleveland clients, Walker and Weeks worked on winter homes for members of the Hanna clan and its entourage near Thomasville, Georgia. They also participated in the Florida boom of the twenties, where the principal protagonist of the original St. Augustine and Miami developments a generation earlier had been Clevelander Henry M. Flagler. On Florida's west coast Walker and Weeks planned a race track in Sarasota for a group of Cleveland businessmen and a grand luxury apartment in St. Petersburg, although neither seems to have materialized.

The two biggest building projects of the twenties in Cleveland went to the Chicago firm of Graham, Anderson, Probst & White. Being overlooked for the giant Union Trust Building in 1923 must have been keenly felt by Walker and Weeks, especially since the bank specialists had planned buildings for five members of the 1920 merger. The largest project of the decade was the grandiose Terminal Tower complex, a $179 million undertaking, but, for whatever reason, Walker and Weeks had no connection with the Van Sweringen developments other than a pair of demonstration homes for Shaker Heights in 1917. A small irony lay in the fact that the Cleveland Play House, designed by the Van Sweringens' favorite architects, Small and Rowley, was built in 1927 on the Francis Drury property for which Walker and Weeks had planned an ambitious garden apartment project that was never built.

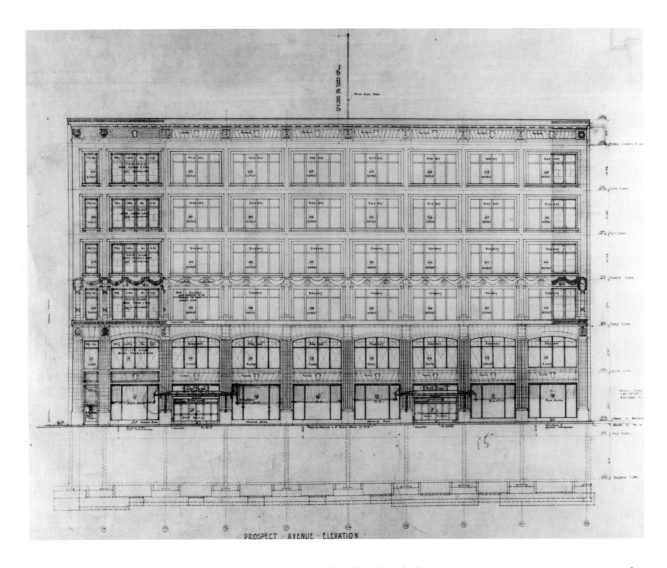

PROSPECT · AVENUE · ELEVATION ·

Halle Building, Prospect-Huron annex, 1926.

When Samuel Halle decided in 1924 to construct an annex to the company's fourteen-year-old Euclid Avenue department store designed by Henry Bacon, architect of the Lincoln Memorial, it was clear that it should match the original building. Walker and Weeks's plans were unveiled in March 1926. The distinguishing details of Bacon's elegant design were repeated on the six-story Huron-Prospect building—crisp, precise terra-cotta detail; graceful segmental arches at the second story, with their simulated voussoirs; and boldly molded garlands above the third story. In addition, the Halles proposed to link the two structures across Huron Road with a two-level bridge at the fourth and fifth floors. The buildings were ninety-nine feet apart, and the bridge would span the street fifty-five feet above the pavement. Walker and Weeks's design shows a light, fanciful arch of Venetian inspiration, topped by an imposing bronze

Halle Building, bridge over Huron Road, version submitted to client, 1926.

clock. It is not unlikely that they referred to the similar bridge at Wanamaker's store in Philadelphia. However, neighboring property owners objected to the bridge and won a court injunction against the Halle Company. Instead, the only link between the buildings was a tunnel, thus creating a continuous 450-foot-long sales aisle between Euclid and Prospect Avenues. The Huron-Prospect building was completed in 1927. Again, the contractor was John Gill & Sons. The store's publicity proudly described the latest communications systems—a profusion of telephone lines, executive intercom systems, and pneumatic tubes for dispatching sales slips and cash.

It is possible that if Samuel Halle had not taken a strong personal hand working with the architects, the detail of the Huron-Prospect building would not have been identical with the Henry Bacon design. This is

Halle Building, art deco version of the bridge over Huron Road, 1926.

suggested by the fact that Walker and Weeks provided an alternate design for the Huron Road bridge of striking geometric lines in the art deco idiom. Apparently the design was not published, however, and it never left the office. But Walker and Weeks had established a continuing relationship with the Halle Brothers Store. They planned branch stores in Canton and Warren, Ohio, in 1928–29, and Samuel H. Halle, one of the original founders in 1891 and still active in 1946, called on them again twenty years later. At first it was proposed to extend the original building to the angled point of Huron Road and Euclid Avenue. Instead, having decided that the triangular plan was uneconomical, the company built a west wing facing on Huron and bridging East 12th Street to connect with the Euclid Avenue building, added three stories to the original 1910 building, and constructed a service building on Prospect next to the Huron-

Halle Building, Point Building addition, 1946–47.

Hollenden Hotel, east wing addition, 1927.

Prospect building. Even in 1946–48, after a generation of depression, war, and modernism, all of these additions once again displayed the same decorative details as the original Henry Bacon building.

Contemporary with the Halle building in 1926, Walker and Weeks planned a $5 million addition to Cleveland's historic Hollenden Hotel on Superior at East 6th Street. The ten-story extension to the east of the existing hotel of 1885 was bedecked with Georgian classical details that

One of a number of designs for the Cleveland Life Insurance Company Building, 1921.

included urns on the roof parapet. The style was not adventurous; it was a comfortable exercise that looked like any other hotel of the period. As it turned out, the old chateauesque building continued to serve until 1962, after which it, together with the Walker and Weeks addition, was demolished to make way for an anonymous vernacular international style hostelry that, in its turn, was torn down in 1989.

Another design for the Cleveland Life
Insurance Company Building, 1921.

One of several designs for the William
Taylor Son and Company Store, 1929.

The transition from classicism to modernism that characterized Walker
and Weeks's bank design was played out again in projected plans for William H. Hunt's Cleveland Life Insurance Company, which proposed to
build on Euclid Avenue one block east of East 30th Street. The firm drew
two schemes between 1921 and 1925. The first was a reiteration of one of
Walker and Weeks's staple bank designs, an eight-story building with a
round-arched entrance, heavy stone rustication, and a classical cornice.
The second scheme, going even beyond the Lima and Fort Wayne banks,
was a thrusting twenty-story shaft of uncompromisingly vertical lines culminating in a stepped spire with a great beacon on top. Neither scheme
was built, as the office tower was canceled when the company was ab-
sorbed by the Sun Life Assurance Company of Canada in 1926.

Schulte United Building, 1929.

It was in a set of brilliant renderings for an unbuilt project in 1929 that Walker and Weeks's efforts on the tall commercial building reached a climax. The William Taylor Son and Company was one of Cleveland's largest department stores, along with Halle's, Higbee's, and the May Company. The existing Taylor Store at 630 Euclid Avenue was already the product of several stages of building by Dyer and Walker and Weeks. A large expansion program was planned, and drawings were made for a building on the same site. The perspective drawings by Wilbur H. Adams, one of the men who produced most of the office's renderings, showed a building filling the entire block between Euclid and Prospect and culminating in a tower. There is little question that Adams's drawings for the Taylor Store were shaped by the visionary renderings of Hugh Ferriss, the great architectural illustrator whose series showing the setback massing of skyscrapers under the New York zoning laws was published in 1922. They emphasized sculptural mass and shape in great building blocks rather than architectural detail. Likewise, the Taylor Store renderings do not show enough detail even to indicate the number of stories; the surroundings suggest that there may have been about twenty-five. The great masses of the Taylor Store step up in four stages in a complex series of ziggurat-like setbacks. The project was greatly reduced in scope by the onset of the depression, but if it had been built, the Taylor Store would have rivaled the Telephone Building, and even parts of the Terminal complex, in its effect on Cleveland's skyline.

The first modernistic design actually executed by Walker and Weeks in downtown Cleveland, the Schulte United Department Store, required the renovation of the Kendall Building, a commercial block built in 1887 across Euclid Avenue from East 6th Street. The building contains the entrance passage of the Colonial Arcade, which had run through to Prospect Avenue since 1898. Both the store interior and the facade were rebuilt in 1929; a step parapet, six fluted piers of granite, and geometric panels of terra-cotta refaced the old building. Perhaps the most fortunate feature of the design was that its position at the foot of East 6th Street formed a new visual focus for the dead-end street.

The impact of the modernistic movement was felt just as strongly in interior design, if not more so. At the same time that Walker and Weeks's concert hall for the Cleveland Orchestra was being completed in 1931, they designed the Lotus Garden, a "dine and dance palace"[24] that incorporated changing light effects like those introduced in the concert hall's color organ. The architects of the late twenties and early thirties were fascinated by the possibilities of dramatic electrical illumination; this interest was most graphically displayed in the world fairs and expositions of the period. The indirect lighting system, dubbed "Colorama," was the most popular feature of the Lotus Garden, which was located on the remodeled second floor of the Guenther Building on Euclid Avenue at East 18th Street. The system permitted constantly changing color effects through the use of primary colors, achieved with red, green, and blue lamps with sets of dimmer controls. The orchestra leader could change the timing of the dimmers to produce any number of color combinations. The dining areas of the Chinese-American restaurant were placed on two sides of the central dance floor; the lights played on the higher ceiling over the dance area. The orchestra platform at the end of the room was brilliantly decorated in red and aluminum tones with Chinese motifs strongly influenced by the prevailing art deco taste, and the side walls of the dining area were decorated with aluminum-finished paper. The Lotus Garden attracted the "cafe society" of the thirties until it closed in 1941, when Walker and Weeks again remodeled the building for the Builders Exchange.

One of a number of designs for the Goodyear Service Station, 1931.

The rapidity with which older academic architects like Walker and Weeks adapted to the developing modernistic style can be measured by the changes between 1925 and 1931. In 1925 Walker and Weeks made their first major departure from the classical tradition with the Lima bank. Six years later they were planning a streamlined "Depression Modern" building for a Goodyear Service Station in Cleveland. An unusual amount of documentation survives for the preliminary design process. The designer, Wilbur Adams, sketched and revised, tried and reflected, arranged and rearranged various modern forms with great abandon. Several ideas were tried for the Goodyear trademark signs, from a massive square sign in stepped planes to a tall vertical pylon with a streamlined profile and the final ninety-foot towers with angular cubist lines. The basic form of the building underwent a similar evolution. One vision of an exterior wall with a concave-convex corner outline was finally transformed into a sweeping curved bay for the window showroom. The complete building was faced with the yellow and blue Goodyear colors, the huge vertical sign was spelled out in blue neon, and the exterior was illuminated with twenty-four floodlights mounted on standards. The 225-foot-long, sleek, three-story building, marked with horizontal bands of windows, would have been at home at the Chicago Century of Progress Exposition in 1933 or Cleveland's own Great Lakes Exposition in 1936. Although its features were those of the international style, the epoch-making Museum of Modern Art exhibition that first introduced a general awareness of the European architects was still more than a year away.

Several things strike the observer of the commercial buildings of Walker and Weeks's era. The department stores, office buildings, retail shops, theaters, restaurants, hotels, and even gas stations of the teens and twenties were the places where most city dwellers of the first half of the century passed their working and living days, yet what is among the most civilized architecture ever built has been all but ignored by the historian. In Cleveland, one is struck by the ubiquitousness of Walker and Weeks's work. It is impossible to walk more than a block or two in the downtown without encountering one of their buildings. Equally noteworthy is the fact that they were called upon to execute commercial work from Massachusetts to Illinois, Michigan to Florida.

In some ways the earliest buildings, before the classical formula took hold, like the Renkert, Bingham, and Goodyear buildings, and the late work, when everyone seemed free to explore the "new architecture," are more interesting to the modern observer. In a world bounded by relatively strict architectural conventions, Walker and Weeks moved with freedom as well as assurance. The designers they assembled were conservative, both in the sense of agreeing with gradual rather than sudden change and of avoiding showiness. But they were also guided by that part of the old precept that says, "Be not the last to lay the old aside." There was always a sense of freshness and vitality to their designs, no matter what the idiom. All of this does not mean that Walker and Weeks were unaware of the advertising function and the need for drawing power of commercial architecture, but they were designing for an era when attractiveness was more likely to be an expression of reputation and goodwill than of marketing and promotion.

Walker and Weeks may be forgiven for the occasional apparent lapse of judgment from the point of view of the latter twentieth century, especially an alteration to the Euclid Avenue facade of the world-famous Cleveland Arcade in 1939. In that case, the spirit of the age was modernization, and the time when the architecture of 1890 would be appreciated was at least thirty years away. Moreover, as one wit has remarked, the first principle of architectural practice is "Get the job!" In this respect, Walker and Weeks had no rivals.

chapter 5

PUBLIC BUILDINGS

Sandusky County Courthouse, Fremont, 1912, reverse print.

WALKER AND WEEKS'S general reputation is largely based on their public buildings. Their success with governmental and civic structures was presaged in a 1912 study for a new Sandusky County Courthouse in Fremont, Ohio. Very likely the proposal came about because of the known work from Dyer's office on the Cleveland City Hall and the Lake and Summit County courthouses. Although it was not executed, the proposed Fremont courthouse was a splendid neoclassic exercise. Two large surviving watercolor renderings in the elegant beaux-arts style of illustration show a monumental two-story building with a frontispiece of four great Corinthian columns and a Roman saucer dome. Recumbent lions and two seated figures flank the entrance; the artist had a delightful sense of humor, for he rendered one of the figures as Michelangelo's Moses and the other as Giuliano de' Medici.

Such major commissions did not come easily to such a young firm. In 1912 Walker and Weeks were given the assignment for an eastside Cleveland police precinct station, and in 1914 they received the commission for the old Cleveland Heights High School, built in 1916; it later became Boulevard Elementary School after the present high school was built in 1925. The basic layout was patterned after an Ashtabula high school whose plans they consulted. The plans are undated but appear to be consistent with those of the Ashtabula Harbor High School built in 1911–12. A study

Cleveland Heights High School, Cleveland
Heights, 1916.

Cleveland Public Library, 1923.

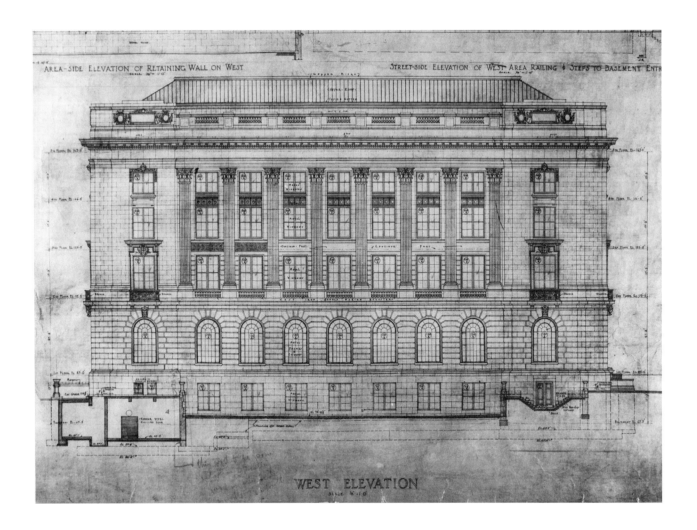

WEST ELEVATION

Cleveland Public Library, 1923, side
elevation.

of the Cleveland Heights schools in 1922 criticized the Tudor-style building as "rather extravagant and indefinite in the use of floor space."[25] (Of course the consultant presented his own plan as the ideal one.) In spite of this hindsight, the high school was in fact a sound and practical, if not elegant, solution in a period of rapidly changing educational philosophy and requirements.

In 1915 an opportunity presented itself that proved to be a turning point in the career of Walker and Weeks: the competition for the Cleveland Public Library building was announced. The site allocated was the block to the east of the U.S. Courthouse occupied by the Case Block, which was about to be vacated by city offices upon the completion of the new city hall. This was one of the key sites in the Mall development that had been under way since Cleveland's Group Plan was adopted in 1903. The comprehensive plan for grouping the city's major public buildings was prepared by the Group Plan Commission consisting of Daniel Burnham,

Arnold W. Brunner, and John M. Carrere. The Federal Building, Cuyahoga County Courthouse, and Cleveland City Hall had been designed by various architects and finished by 1916. A building large enough to complement the federal building, whose location at the south end of the Mall was one of the determining elements in the plan, had always been contemplated. Arnold Brunner designed the Federal Building, and his model was the pair of eighteenth-century facades on the Place de la Concorde in Paris. Burnham and his associates had visited Paris while preparing the plan for Washington, D.C., in 1901 and noted the similarities between the Concorde and the requirements of the Group Plan. Fifty-eight architectural firms expressed an interest in entering the library competition. A. D. F. Hamlin of Columbia University's School of Architecture was chosen as juror and eight firms were selected. Each competitor received an honorarium of one thousand dollars. Besides Walker and Weeks, two Cleveland architects were chosen, Abram Garfield and Hubbell & Benes. The other competitors were John Russell Pope, best known later as the architect of the Jefferson Memorial and the National Gallery of Art; Edward L. Tilton, architect of the Ellis Island Immigration Station and Cleveland's Carnegie West Library (1910); Robert D. Kohn, New York architect of the Lindner Building in Cleveland; Allen & Collins, designers of New York's Riverside Church and Union Theological Seminary; and Holabird & Roche, winners of the commission for the Chicago City Hall–Cook County Building in 1905. Formidable competition! But in August 1916, two independent juries in Cleveland and New York chose Walker and Weeks's plan. The beginning of construction was delayed by the war and its increased costs. A second bond issue was passed in 1921, however, and the building was finally erected in 1922–25.

With the Group Plan guidelines, the famous Paris square, and the completed Federal Building as precedents, the chief direction for the new building was clearly established. The winning design was nearly identical in height, size, shape, and general style to the Federal Building but had subtle and complementary differences in its details. The five-story building has the same arcaded ground story, the same colossal colonnades for the middle stories, and the same cornice height. The library's functions demanded more daylight, and the plan achieved a 40 percent greater window area. The interiors were designed in a classical Renaissance manner like those of the county courthouse and city hall. The vaulted lobby and main reading room are truly monumental public spaces on a Roman scale.

Their beaux-arts training in symmetry, order, the procession of ceremonial spaces, and the grouping of functions in a hierarchical system, with careful attention to the transitions between them, served the architects

Cleveland Public Auditorium, 1916–28.

well. The functional elements of the design were widely praised, and they established a precedent for many subsequent library buildings. The plan was decentralized, which was only one of the approaches to planning common in the American library tradition since the late nineteenth century. One of the other types, for example, consisted of a tall central reading hall surrounded by several stories of balconies with stacks; Harvard and Yale had such libraries. Another type was characterized by a massive storage block of closed stacks, exemplified by the Library of Congress and the Boston Public Library. The decentralized type consisted of a series of rooms or departments with all of the shelving available to the user. This type had been advocated by William Frederick Poole in 1881 and applied in the building of the Newberry Library in Chicago (1888–93). In Poole's ideal plan the various rooms were accessible from an interior hallway around a central court. This was the plan adopted in the Cleveland Public Library. There were fifteen reading rooms for various subjects, all located on the periphery for daylight, with their stacks concentrated around the central court. The amount of open stack space available to the public

Cleveland Public Auditorium, 1916–28, model of interior.

was revolutionary. With forty-seven miles of shelving, its capacity was the third largest in the country. The arrangement of the various departments and the provisions for circulation, storage, and retrieval were efficiently and painstakingly planned. Walker and Weeks's designer for the plan was apparently Claude W. Stedman. Twenty years later Walker wrote, "Our library building is recognized as a new point of departure in library planning for a reference library. Oxford, when planning a new library, sent their architect, son of Sir Gilbert Scott, to spend some time in Cleveland, and Los Angeles embraced our arrangement of relation of stack to readers for their building."[26] The achievement of a masterful solution within the requirements of the Group Plan established Walker and Weeks as architects whose civic work was equal in every respect to their commercial buildings.

Three major structures within the Group Plan boundaries had not appeared in the original plan, and Walker and Weeks were connected with all of them. The need for a large public auditorium and convention hall was realized early in the century, and in that same year, 1916, the hall was financed by a bond issue. Although planning and design started immediately, construction did not begin until 1920, and the Public Auditorium was dedicated in 1922. A Music Hall seating 2,800 was added to the south end of the auditorium in 1928. The architects of the auditorium were city architects Frederic H. Betz and J. Harold McDowell, and Frank Walker was employed as consulting architect. Their respective roles are not documented

The Public Auditorium was the largest such convention hall in the country at the time of its completion. Over 300 feet long, the auditorium has a clear span of 215 feet. The combined seating capacity of the main floor and the long U-shaped galleries is over 11,500. In spite of its size, the acoustical properties are excellent. The basement exhibition hall contained more than 28,500 square feet of exhibit space and was accessible by numerous ramps and stairways. The circulation plan was designed so that 13,000 people could be evacuated from the building in four and a half minutes.

The style of the building is Italian Renaissance, and the auditorium achieves a classical simplicity with its wide ceiling of curving arches. The entrance lobby shows an impressive, if somewhat heavy, use of classical ornament executed in marble, tile, and decorative plaster. On the exterior, the problem of making architectural sense of such vast stretches of wall was admirably handled by the arrangement of the arcaded windows, the high rusticated podium, and the cornice line that conformed to the requirements of the Group Plan.

At the end of the twenties, Walker and Weeks planned the building completing the east side of the Mall, the Board of Education Administration Building. The six-story sandstone building, with three wings forming an E-shape on East 6th Street, is essentially a large public office building. The placement of a bronze statue of Lincoln by Max Kalish on the Mall side of the building was the result of several years' effort (in which Walker and Weeks were involved) to create a Lincoln memorial somewhere in the city. In the summer of 1930, the *Plain Dealer* and the *Cleveland Press* chose to make a political issue (political because of the stone supplier's connections) of the fact that sandstone was chosen instead of the limestone, granite, or marble of the other Group Plan buildings. At the same time, an even more damning criticism was leveled by a local magazine: "All [the Mall buildings] are but cemetery burying vaults on a big scale. The Public Auditorium is a splendid exception. School headquarters, we are afraid, will not be."[27]

In fact, the exterior design suggests certain compromises. In order to conform to the cornice height prescribed by the Group Plan, the main

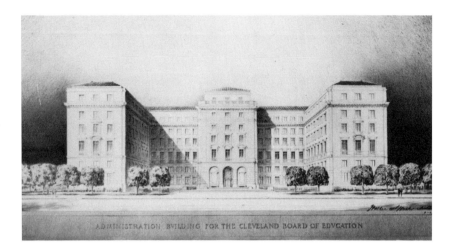

Cleveland Board of Education, Administration Building, 1916–28, East 6th Street elevation, 1930.

Cleveland Board of Education, Administration Building, 1916–28, Mall elevation, 1930.

cornice is at the fifth story, so that the sixth floor looks like an afterthought. Moreover, the classical detail lacks vigor, especially when compared with the robust neighboring Public Library. Walker himself had clearly identified the design challenge at the beginning. "This is primarily a utilitarian building in a group of as monumental structures as any in the city. Our problem has been to reconcile these two considerations."[28] But the best work of Walker and Weeks by 1922–25 was making the transition to the new nonhistorical idiom, and it seems certain that without the constraints of the Group Plan formula the Board of Education building would have been less classical.

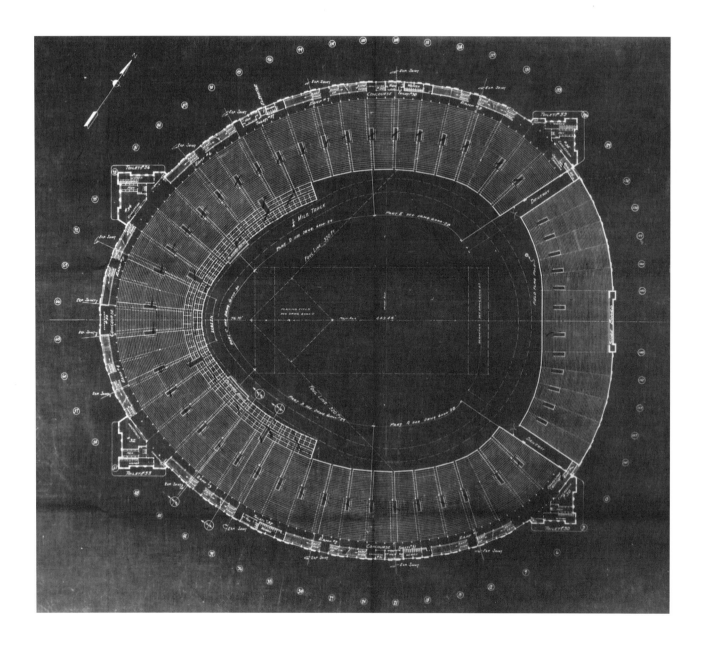

Lakefront (Cleveland Municipal) Stadium, 1929–30.

Another major structure that had not been dreamed of in 1903, a municipal stadium, was located on the lakefront and considered a complement to the Group Plan. As spectator sports became more and more popular after the war, planning for a stadium began in the mid-twenties under the sponsorship of City Manager William Hopkins. It was planned to be a great city-owned multipurpose facility for sports, conventions, concerts, and public gatherings. A bond issue was passed in 1928, construction began in 1930, and the first event was held in the new stadium on July 3, 1931.

The completed structure had permanent seating for 78,000, and with chairs placed on the field this was increased to 92,000. The plan was oval in shape, with the superstructure open at the east end. The stadium covered an area of twelve acres, enclosing a four-acre playing field. The outer walls were made of a mottled gray brick with terra-cotta trim. The engineering design was executed by the Osborn Engineering Company, which had built a reputation as stadium designers, having planned more than seventy-five since 1900, including New York's Yankee Stadium, Boston's Fenway Park, and Chicago's Comiskey Park.

Walker and Weeks were responsible for the architectural design. The planning of amphitheaters has been subject to architectural treatment since the days of the Romans, but it is significant that the design of the Cleveland stadium was *not* historical. The 116-foot-tall structure (ten stories) featured a number of devices used to minimize the height. The outer brick wall was only sixty-one feet tall, and the superstructure of steel and aluminum was set back above the walls. The superstructure's aluminum louvered facing and roof were intended to reflect the color of the sky, making them appear less obtrusive when viewed against the lake. The use of structural aluminum was one of the earliest in the country and the most extensive to that date, comprising 130,000 pounds of aluminum. Four masonry-faced towers that functioned as entrances and booths were architecturally necessary "visually to anchor [the structure] to the ground."[29] Such visual considerations help to explain the role of the architect working on a structure that might be considered strictly utilitarian. It is doubtful that many such structures show the subtle artistic considerations expressed by Frank Walker.

The completion of the stadium inspired an article by Armen H. Tashjian, Walker and Weeks's chief engineer, on the use of metal for exterior walls. The article reviewed the historical transition from the masonry bearing-wall to the "curtain wall" and was an excellent statement of the application of logic and rationalism in twentieth-century architecture. Tashjian cited the tower of the Chrysler Building and wall sections of the Empire State Building as contemporary examples, pointing up the importance of the advanced use of aluminum on the stadium.[30]

The principal monumental civic building that occupied Walker and Weeks for many years was, however, not in Cleveland, not even in Ohio, but in neighboring Indiana. At the end of World War I, a memorial was proposed to all those Hoosiers who had served and died in the war. It was envisioned as being part of a park or plaza in the heart of the state capital, Indianapolis. The general assembly created the Indiana World War Memorial in 1920. The state, county, and city set aside a tract of five city blocks for the enormous project. The board of trustees of the memorial wrote the program on which a nationwide competition was based. Some

Indiana World War Memorial, Indianapolis, 1927.

Indiana World War Memorial, 1927, site plan.

twenty-two firms submitted plans. Thomas R. Kimball served as the architectural adviser to the board. The jury consisted of Henry Bacon, architect of the Lincoln Memorial (and Cleveland's Halle store); Milton B. Medary of Philadelphia, architect of the Bok Carillon and collaborator with Paul Cret on the Detroit Institute of Arts; and Charles Platt, architect of the Freer Gallery in Washington and perhaps the greatest student of the Italian Renaissance style in America. Walker and Weeks were declared the winners in 1923.

The great plaza in the center of Indianapolis is five hundred feet wide and a half-mile long, half again as long as the Cleveland Mall, whose

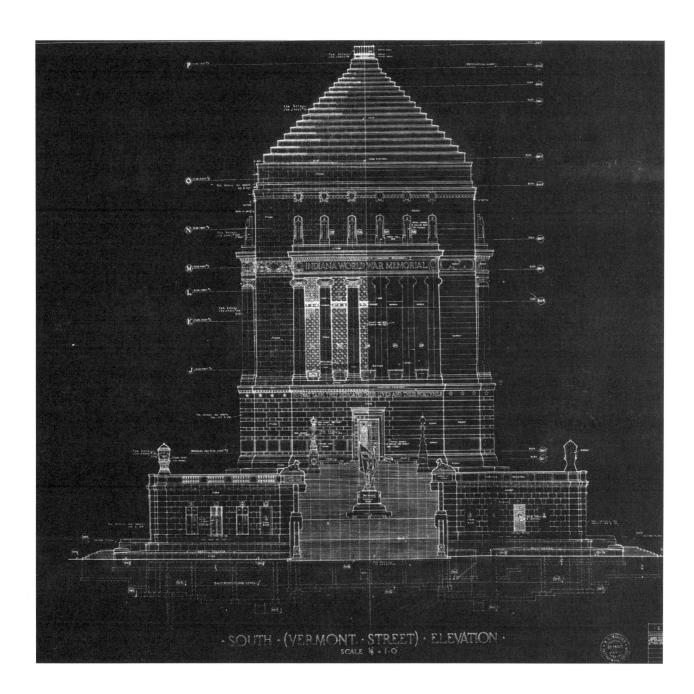

· SOUTH · (VERMONT · STREET) · ELEVATION ·
SCALE ⅛ = 1'-0"

Indiana World War Memorial, 1927.

open space had not yet been cleared of buildings in the early 1920s. The principles of Daniel Burnham's plan—symmetry, order, and uniformity—were firmly in the architects' minds during the design process. From north to south, the five blocks of the plaza contain a sunken garden and cenotaph, a terraced esplanade with walks and geometrical plantings, an open square with an obelisk and fountain, the main Memorial Shrine, and a circular plaza with gardens and another fountain. Facing the north end of the plaza is the public library and at the south end the Federal Building, both neoclassic structures. And symmetrically placed on either side of the cenotaph square are buildings for the national home of the American Legion. While Memorial Plaza was considered substantially complete in 1937, the last of the American Legion buildings was not finished until 1948.

It is nearly impossible, after almost seventy years, to enter into the spirit in which the Indiana World War Memorial was created. The entire conception was one of the last in which patriotic and spiritual symbolism were derived from the style and forms of classical architecture. Certainly by World War II that impulse was almost completely vitiated. The closest equivalent in modern times is the Vietnam Memorial, but the nature of its stark abstract form is light-years from the literary symbolism and classical vocabulary of the 1920s.

On the northernmost square, the black granite cenotaph, a tribute to the war dead, is flanked by four black columns surmounted by stylized gilded eagles that symbolize America's participation in the war. In the obelisk square, a hundred-foot black granite shaft was intended to represent the hopes and aspirations of the nation for renewed life. Its fountain played at night with illuminated jets.

The architects based the design of the shrine building itself, which was erected in 1926–28, on the Mausoleum of Halicarnassus, an accepted classical pattern for a monumental tomb structure. The Hellenistic building, one of the wonders of the ancient world, was the subject of conjectural reconstructions by various scholars. In one of these there was believed to have been a rectangular podium approximately 82 by 116 feet, supporting a temple with thirty-six 40-foot-tall Ionic columns and topped by a pyramid. The Indiana shrine is 106 feet square, with six Ionic columns on each 45-foot-tall face, and a pyramidal roof. On the south staircase, placed on a base of pink granite, is the statue *Pro Patria*, the largest bronze casting ever made in America at the time. A nude male youth strides forward carrying the unfurled American flag, "suggesting that love of beauty, liberty, and the spirit of sacrifice for the preservation of our ideals, must not die."[31]

The total height of the shrine building above the street is 210 feet, but the scale of the structure is difficult to appreciate until one is confronted by the grand staircases inside that lead from the foyer to the Shrine Room. Each staircase climbs nearly 40 feet between floors, the equivalent of more than three stories. Upon entering the Shrine Room at the top of the stairs, the modern viewer's first impression is one of awe and incredulity. Twenty-four giant red granite pillars with stylized composite capitals range around the 84-foot square room. Between them a deep blue light filters

Columbus Memorial Lighthouse Competition, Dominican Republic, 1927–29.

into the room from twenty stained-glass windows. The recessed ceiling is spangled with starlike electric lights. In the center of the room is the Altar of Consecration flanked by four Roman torcheres. A series of niches around the room contain portraits of the leading soldiers from every front, and above a 17-foot marble wainscot is an allegorical sculptured frieze depicting America joining the Allies, the great struggle, and the realization of peace.

The stated purpose of the Shrine Room is "to inspire good citizenship."[32] In the secularism and disillusion of the late twentieth century, it is difficult to appreciate fully all of the intended symbolism. The aesthetic effect and the general style make almost irresistible the observation that the room recalls the gaudy lobby of a movie palace. This is not necessarily a derogatory comparison, since the function of the room is not dissimilar: to transport the observer to another sphere. The totality inspires a conviction of the utter seriousness of the creators of the memorial, and the viewer leaves genuinely moved.

Many talents collaborated on such a monumental work. Henry Hering was the sculptor of *Pro Patria* and worked with Walker and Weeks on many other projects, as did Frank Jirouch, sculpture of the Shrine Room frieze and partner in Fischer and Jirouch. At least three of Walker and Weeks's designers are identified with the memorial design—J. Byers Hays, Dana Clark, and Edwin J. Truthan—yet Frank Walker must still be seen as the controlling intellect overseeing all of these talents.

The strain of gorgeous theatricality that appeared in the Indiana shrine reached its full flowering in yet another memorial competition; one, however, in which Walker and Weeks were unsuccessful. The proposed monument was a lighthouse on the island of Hispaniola, where Columbus first landed in the New World. Initially conceived in the nineteenth century and revived in 1914 and again in 1923, the idea of a memorial to Columbus finally resulted in a competition in 1927 sponsored by the Pan American Union and the government of the Dominican Republic. The first stage of the competition brought entries from 455 architects representing forty-eight countries. Meeting in Madrid in April 1929, the jury, which included Raymond Hood and Eliel Saarinen, selected ten preliminary finalists who were given two years to revise and complete their proposals. The jury met again in Rio de Janeiro and chose the design of J. L. Gleave of Manchester, England, a long, recumbent, cross-shaped structure.

Walker and Weeks's entry (No. 162) did not pass the first stage, but their design was a fascinating scheme that epitomized the richness, audacity, and color of the twenties. The renderings submitted to the jury were alive with atmosphere, executed in watercolor and India ink for a sumptuous effect. At the western approach to the memorial, a series of monumental staircases led to a platform where, on a pedestal, a bronze statue of Columbus carrying a flag aloft stood, not unlike the *Pro Patria*. It was flanked by two 300-foot octagonal pylons, and beyond them, towering more than 550 feet, was the lighthouse shaft. The ornamentation of the structure was profuse and colorful, largely geometric in form, and drew freely on pre-Columbian Indian motifs. The dominantly zigzag and setback shapes show all too clearly how pre-Columbian ornament was a major source for the art deco style. Behind the tower, the structure was built up in stepped masses like Mayan or Aztec pyramids. A series of interior chambers, culminating in an octagonal chapel where the remains of Columbus would be deposited, were exercises in the gothic, Spanish baroque, and Renaissance styles. In front of the memorial, crowds of people were depicted, adding color, movement, and vitality to the drawing of the colossal structure.

In spite of the monumental character, there is a "tongue-in-cheek" aspect to the representation. The spirit of a Hollywood epic is all too evident. Moreover, there is a striking similarity between the basic concept of the tapered shaft surrounded by pinnacles and a published student project for a hypothetical monument to Louis Sullivan. The project appeared in the *Journal of the American Institute of Architects* in December 1928 (a copy of which exists in Walker and Weeks's files), only months before the competition entries were due in Madrid. This does not necessarily raise the issue of plagiarism, but it does illustrate the fact that in an eclectic climate all sources, whether historical or contemporary, were fair game. Nevertheless, although the seriousness of the Columbus competition design may be questioned, it remains an example of the symbolism and monumentalism that reached a climax in the Indiana World War Memorial. These elements continued to reappear, in an increasingly enervated state, throughout the thirties, but never again with the scale and solemnity of these monuments.

By the end of the twenties, the new stylized nonhistorical idiom was developing simultaneously in monumental public buildings and commercial office buildings. Penelope Redd, writing on the completion of the Pittsburgh branch of the Cleveland Federal Reserve Bank in 1931, observed that "an unprejudiced review of this structure requires a complete readjustment on the part of all familiar with classic architecture as the archetype for buildings of this character." The free-standing building with strong vertical piers was faced with light-gray Georgia marble, and the window frames and ornamental spandrels were all of extruded or cast aluminum. Redd pointed out that "as we usually see masonry it has a structural quality. However, the modern point of view is different. Masonry no longer does any work. The steel frame supports the building. Masonry is but a veneer."[33]

Harrison County Courthouse, Clarksburg, West Virginia, 1931.

The interiors of the bank were of marble, travertine, black Carrara glass, and metal trim, and the floors were of terrazzo. Redd compared the building to a gleaming casket of marble bound with aluminum. "The sensation of viewing a highly decorative treasure chest is further emphasized by the heavy aluminum plates which make the penthouse the lid of the casket."[34] The use of aluminum on the penthouse story made a wall of extreme lightness and, together with rock-wool insulation, achieved an insulating value as great as a masonry wall ten times thicker. Tashjian's article on the exterior use of architectural metals discussed the aluminum walls in detail. Compared with the Federal Reserve Bank in Cleveland, conceived as a Renaissance fortress, the Pittsburgh building, hous-

United States Post Office, Cleveland, 1932.

ing the same function, vividly demonstrated the stylistic evolution of the late twenties.

Likewise, a county courthouse might be more like a contemporary office building than a similar public building a decade earlier. A description of the Harrison County Courthouse in Clarksburg, West Virginia, written in 1932 by Ruth F. Stone, Walker and Weeks's public relations editor, extolled the simplicity of expression as contrasted with the old classical forms for public buildings. It went on to point out that the new design still expressed the required "strength, security, and dignity."[35] Mentioned with pride was the absence of the long ceremonial flight of steps associated with older classical buildings; it has an entrance nearly at grade level. The masonry veneer walls covering the structural steel frame are of buff Indiana limestone and polished black granite, and the decorative metal on the exterior is a lead- or tin-based white metal.

The simplified geometric forms of the style were not inhospitable to the classically trained architect. The new idiom was symmetrical, the building masses (as distinct from the ornamental treatment) were handled in a way appropriate to the traditional use of masonry, and the style provided for the use of sculptural embellishment. The architectural design was one of balance and order that still embraced beaux-arts principles, but it differed in the geometric simplification and frank use of surface ornament. Walker and Weeks's regular collaborator Henry Hering executed the sculptural ornament for both the Pittsburgh Federal Reserve Bank building and the Clarksburg courthouse. Conventionalized eagles and low-relief figures summarized the character of what Ruth Stone called "a distinct stylized design"; the terms "art deco" and "art moderne" were not yet current.

The last of Walker and Weeks's major public buildings was the United States Post Office in Cleveland. This new federal building was planned in the late 1920s, before the onset of the Great Depression, but it was not actually constructed until 1933–34. The official architect was James A. Wetmore of the Treasury office in Washington; most post offices were designed by the regular staff of the supervising Architect of the U.S. Treasury Department. Walker and Weeks were engaged as the local and de facto architects in the spring of 1931; correspondence between Frank Walker and Congressman Chester C. Bolton indicates that the latter was probably influential in the awarding of the contract. The project was such a large and complex one that Walker and Weeks entered into an association with Philip L. Small & Associates—architects of Shaker Square, the Cleveland Play House, and John Carroll University—to complete the work. In order to keep the operation of the associated architects (one a partnership and the other a corporation) distinct from their individual businesses, a joint office was set up for the combined operation. It was housed in an annex at 2404 Prospect Avenue that was actually an extension of the 2341 Carnegie Avenue building. The operation had its own staff drawn from the other two offices, including a chief designer and a project manager; structural, mechanical, and electrical engineers; specification writers; junior designers; and architectural and engineering draftsmen. The staff submitted the first "cabinet sketches" and estimates for the building to the federal government in October 1931.

The site was to be in the Cleveland Union Terminal group, and the external design was intended to harmonize with the terminal buildings. Frank Walker and Philip Small stated that their assignment was to design a building "as monumental as is consistent with its essentially utilitarian purpose,"[36] but Walker also said that he understood that it was not to be monumental in the same sense that the old federal building and the public library were. The five-story rectangular block was articulated with fluted piers between each rank of windows, and ornament was used very sparingly. The engineering design was complicated by the fact that the building was erected on the air rights over the railroad tracks on the western approach to the terminal and required a complex cantilevered structure. Because of the site, a unique system for chutes and conveyors was designed to carry mail directly to and from the railroad platforms. When completed, the new federal building housed other departments besides the U.S. Post Office, including the Veterans Administration and the Civil Service Commission. The only public space was the 228-foot-long lobby stretching between Prospect and Huron.

During the entire design process, the Cleveland architects conferred frequently with federal officials. Because so many buildings were constructed in the new simplified style by the federal government in the thirties, there is a tendency to speak of an official government style. In fact, according to writers summarizing the federal building program at the end of the decade, traditional design predominated. On the other hand, they noted that:

> The designers of public works . . . have borrowed much from the general current that is flowing away from traditional design toward something new, but in reviewing their work from a close perspective it seems very evident that they have decidedly contributed to the movement. . . . Most of the architects who have attempted to diverge from tradition seem to have attacked their problems from the point of view first of plan requirements, secondly of construction, and thirdly of type of materials to be used, with the result that in the more successful buildings of this character a style has emerged that may perhaps be the seed of the long sought "school of American design."[37]

The notion of a "school of American design" or a "new architecture" is one that had a great deal of currency in the late thirties and forties. Walker gave utterance to the idea on more than one occasion, although it is not entirely clear how much Walker and Weeks considered their work to be a part of the trend. What is clear is that for two decades they dominated the field of public architecture in Cleveland and a large portion of the Midwest. Earlier architects had made a specialty of courthouses and other public buildings in the period just before and after the turn of the century, as did others during the great period of federal public works during the depression. But the twenties, in particular, were the years when many cities, especially in the industrial northeast, reached their ultimate size, were taking their final physical shape, and built the monumental structures that put the mark of civilization on that city. The heroic neoclassical style approved and fostered by beaux-arts training was the natural style for the new metropolitan image. Walker and Weeks not only brought the right talents to the right commissions, but they were at the right place at the right time. The half-dozen major public buildings that established the permanent physical image of the city of Cleveland in the twenties (not including the Terminal Tower, of course) all came from their office, and these alone would probably have been sufficient to establish Walker and Weeks's general reputation.

In some respects, discussing the architecture of public and institutional buildings separately is artificial. Many of their uses were parallel and overlapping (e.g., public and private education), so it might be expected that their architectural expression would be related. If the former includes government buildings or civic structures for public benefit that are nonfunctional in the utilitarian sense (like the memorials), we can see a clear distinction between them and the institutions that provide similar services or activities but are generally private, nonprofit organizations. It is not surprising to find that Walker and Weeks enjoyed a wide practice in that sphere as well.

chapter 6

INSTITUTIONAL
PLANNING

T HE PREPONDERANCE OF Walker and Weeks's work in the classical
tradition and their performance with discriminating clients recommended them to every kind of private institution. Their work on institutional buildings began promisingly in 1913–14 with St. Vincent's Charity
Hospital in Cleveland. Having been established at its East 22d Street location since 1865, the hospital made a major addition of a new five-story
surgical wing. Each floor has the typical hospital layout of an axial corridor flanked by rooms. The basement contained a dispensary for the poor,
an X-ray department, an emergency room, and a contagious ward. The
first through the fourth floors housed wards of various sizes and some
private rooms. On the fifth floor were consultation and operating rooms,
and contemporary descriptions emphasized the modernity of the mechanical systems.[38] The exterior design, still visible on Central Avenue in 1997,
is of red brick with a fifth-story terra-cotta colonnade. At the same time
Rainbow Cottage (founded in 1887 as Rainbow Hospital for Crippled
and Convalescent Children) built the first unit of its new hospital in South
Euclid, Ohio. Walker and Weeks gave it a two-story stucco building with
end gables related to some of their residential designs.

In 1919 Warner and Swasey, Cleveland's leading manufacturer of machine tools and precision instruments, as well as the telescopes for the
renowned Lick and Yerkes Observatories, asked Walker and Weeks to plan
the astronomical observatory for the Case School of Applied Science on
an elevated site in East Cleveland. Five years earlier they had designed a
small classical pavilion to house the company's nine-inch refracting telescope for the Palace of Machinery at the Panama-Pacific Exposition in
San Francisco. The new observatory was built in two stages. The original
wing at the south end of the structure consisted of a dome supported on a
cylindrical brick tower. The dome was an old one that had been used for
twenty-five years on the property at Worcester Warner's and Ambrose
Swasey's residences on Euclid Avenue. In his presentation address for the
observatory in 1920, Ambrose Swasey said, "This building, because of its
admirable design and construction, tells its own story as to the purpose for

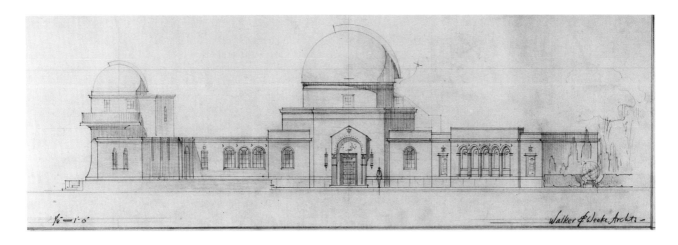

Warner and Swasey Observatory, East
Cleveland, 1919.

which it was erected, and to Messrs. Walker and Weeks, the architects,
and Messrs. Crowell and Little, the builders, too much credit cannot be
given."[39]

Such a building is a good example of the ingenuity of the academic
architect in finding a historical precedent for any functional form. The
dome had, of course, a respectable lineage going back to Rome, the Middle
Ages, and the Renaissance. An initial scheme interpreted Bramante's
Tempietto, with a dome surrounded by a colonnade, as the base for the
observatory; the little sixteenth-century Roman building was the most obvious classical prototype for a small domed structure. This design was
supplanted by a much less elaborate conception, and the entrance porch
and the round-arched windows of the small projecting wing were taken
from Lombard Romanesque architecture. Twenty years later, in 1939, when
the building was enlarged with a twenty-eight-foot dome for a twenty-
four-inch Schmidt telescope, an auditorium, and an exhibit hall, the new
major entrance repeated the motif of the Lombardic round-arched porch.

Walker and Weeks left their greatest imprint on the institutions of Cleveland at the cultural center at University Circle. Although Western Reserve University and the Case School of Applied Science had been located there since the 1880s and the Western Reserve Historical Society
since 1898, it was not until the completion of the Cleveland Museum of
Art in 1916 that the prospect of concentrating the city's cultural institutions in the Wade Park/University district was envisioned. The museum's
architects, Hubbell and Benes, made several sketches and master plans
for the cultural institutions on formal axes in an informal parklike setting.
A University Improvement Company was formed in 1918, partly under
the aegis of Benjamin Hubbell, for preserving the neighborhood and land
values in the Wade Park area. By the early twenties the company controlled most of the property on the east side of East 107th Street from Park

Park Drive Apartment, East 107th
Street, 1916.

Lane to a block south of Euclid Avenue. Its influence extended east along
Euclid Avenue to the present site of the University Hospitals, and a height
limit of four stories was agreed upon.

Walker and Weeks had already designed at least half a dozen residences
in the Wade Park Allotment. They had drawn plans in 1916 for a luxury
apartment house in the French chateau style to be located on East 107th
Street above the lagoon and the park drive that was renamed Liberty Boulevard after World War I (now Martin Luther King Jr. Boulevard). It was

Epworth-Euclid United Methodist Church, 1928.

not built, however, and the property became the site of the most prominent visual landmark in University Circle, Epworth-Euclid United Methodist Church. Walker and Weeks became the principal architects for the project as a consequence of the untimely death of the great ecclesiastical architect Bertram Goodhue in April 1924. Walker and Weeks were involved in the conceptual design as consulting architects from the beginning, although the central conception of the church was evidently Goodhue's. The early sketches of a nave church that widens into a great central octagon with a slender gothic fleche show simple masses with little detail. After Goodhue's death, the definition of the building program continued through 1925 with Walker and Weeks at the center of the discussions between Goodhue's firm and the church.

Many commentators have found a resemblance to Mont St. Michel in the shape of the building and its position dominating the lower boulevard. However, Claude Stedman's description of the finished building

Epworth-Euclid United Methodist Church, view, ca. 1930.

stated that the chief historical reference was the English gothic style, but he made the more important point that the historical style was a point of departure only and that the final design was thoroughly modern, especially in its ornamental sculpture. Honesty and permanence of construction were considered especially important for a church structure, and the church walls were built of solid masonry, with concrete and steel for the floors and roof. The gothic detail is only suggestive, with no flying buttresses, crockets, or finials and with only a minimum of tracery. The sculptured figures by Leo Friedlander, who also executed sculptural ornament for Rockefeller Center, grow out of massive blocks of masonry, becoming more three-dimensional and less planar toward the top. Construction began in 1926, and the church was dedicated in 1928.

At the same time, Walker and Weeks were planning a building for the Cleveland Medical Library Association adjacent to the university campus. The building was to house a library that would document and instruct physicians in the practice of medicine as a humanistic discipline. Walker and Weeks were chosen because their mastery of the classical styles was seen to be appropriate for the concept of medicine as both scientific and humanistic. The building is based on Italian Renaissance and French neoclassic models. Noting the differentiation of story heights through the different sizes of the windows, Michael Partington

Allen Memorial Medical Library, 1924–27.

has suggested that one of the design sources may have been the Petit Trianon at Versailles.[40] The library stands on an open site and thus has four fully developed facades. Georgia marble and Indiana limestone enhance the restrained classicism of the exterior, which Mary-Peale Schofield refers to as having "dignity without pomp, [and] quiet decoration without fuss."[41] The exterior belies the richness of treatment of the interior spaces. The two-story stair hall is faced with buff marble, and the staircase balustrade is finely wrought in iron. The high-ceilinged library and reading rooms have something of the atmosphere of an English university and something of a gentlemen's club. Completed in 1926, the building was named the Allen Memorial Medical Library after Dr. Dudley P. Allen.

Between 1925 and 1927 there was an orgy of planning by institutions either already situated or planning to locate at University Circle. The Western Reserve Historical Society made plans to enlarge its East 107th

Allen Memorial Medical Library, Members'
(H. H. Powell) Reading Room, 1924–27.

Allen Memorial Medical Library, Cushing
Reading Room, 1924–27.

Street museum and library, with Hubbell and Benes, members of the firm that originally designed the building, as architects. The Musical Arts Association was considering a home for the Cleveland Orchestra. Three other institutions engaged Walker and Weeks to prepare plans for buildings that would line the entire east side of East Boulevard facing the lagoon across from the Epworth-Euclid Church. The corner on Euclid was owned by the First Church of Christ, Scientist, for whom Hubbell and Benes had made several studies of squares, circles, and polygons for the 1921 church building. In 1926 Walker and Weeks designed an octagonal domed structure with a columned portico that bore a striking resemblance to the Musical Arts Association's concert hall that was actually built there. North of the church property the Cleveland Museum of Natural History, then located in the Leonard Hanna mansion on Euclid Avenue, planned in 1925 a large building that included a museum, planetarium, and observatory; the Roman style again provided the precedent for the domed structure. The Cleveland School of Art, already occupying a twenty-year-old building in the Wade Park Allotment, had new plans drawn in 1927 for a large facility at the corner of East Boulevard and Bellflower, where in fact the Cleveland Institute of Art did build in 1956. Walker and Weeks proposed a building whose plan was a wide, splayed "U" in shape, with its closed end addressing the corner. None of the three plans prepared by Walker and Weeks was executed.

In 1927 members of the six major institutions—representing the university, art, music, history, natural history, and art education—formed a University Circle Planning Commission. Its purpose was to develop a master plan for the district and to solicit its endorsement by the various institutions. Frank Walker and Abram Garfield, assigned the task of developing a plan, were both chosen because of their roles in Cleveland city planning: Garfield was a member of the Group Plan Commission, and Walker had been technical advisor to the Cleveland City Plan Commission since 1918. Late in 1928 Walker and Garfield presented their tentative group layout for University Circle to President Vinson of Western Reserve University.

The most striking thing about the plan at first glance is the density of the development. It was evidently assumed that the entire Case School/Western Reserve University/Lakeside Hospital group south of Euclid Avenue would be solidly built up with new buildings. Case School and Western Reserve University maintained their separate identities, and the three campuses were linked with formal axes and cross-axes that would create a series of enclosed quadrangles on the north-south axis and an open esplanade west to east. The plan envisioned the removal of some older structures that today would be considered worth saving, such as the original Western Reserve building of 1882, Adelbert Hall, and existing private housing within the area. One noteworthy proposal that was never carried out was the complete bridging of the railroad tracks south of the campuses and the construction of university buildings over them.

North of Euclid Avenue the major buildings proposed by Walker and Weeks—the orchestra hall (on the Euclid corner site purchased by the university from the Christian Science church in 1927), the natural history museum, and the art school—were shown occupying their prominent positions along East Boulevard facing the Fine Arts Garden and lagoon. The scheme did not foresee the expansion of institutions or offices into the residential areas north of the art museum, however; they were still occupied by well-to-do families. In fact, Walker and Weeks had just completed the last of the large Wade Park mansions there in 1921–22, an Italian Renaissance villa for Prentiss Baldwin (with whom Walker was working so closely on the revival of Gates Mills) in the present site of the Cleveland Institute of Music.

The extension of Chester Avenue to the traffic circle intersection of Euclid Avenue was indicated in the plan, although it was not accomplished until after World War II. In hindsight, one of the most remarkable things about the plan was that there was apparently no provision for private automobile parking. The area was well served by streetcar lines, and the complete victory of private transportation was not anticipated.

In general, the existing buildings and the limited remaining space imposed such restrictions that the opportunities for visionary ideas or proposals were few. Within those limits, the plan imposed rigid order that turned out not to be achievable, in view of the haphazard growth of the institutions, the onset of the depression, and new and altered ideas about education, museums, and urban design in the wake of World War II.

At the end of 1928 the Musical Arts Association announced the gift that made possible the architectural keystone of University Circle. Severance Hall is not only one of Walker and Weeks's major architectural triumphs; its design and construction further illuminate the relationship between the architect and a particular breed of donor—the last of the nineteenth-century industrialist-entrepreneurs. Much preliminary thought had been given to the location and the design of the concert hall well before John L. Severance, the founder, financier, and director of many enterprises and president of the Musical Arts Association, announced his million-dollar gift in December 1928. President Vinson showed Severance the tentative layout of the property by Walker and Garfield. Walter McCornack, Cleveland Board of Education architect for 1912 to 1925,

Severance Hall, auditorium, 1929–30.

Severance Hall, 1929–30.

Severance Hall, grand foyer, 1929–30.

had prepared a plan and presented it to Adella Prentiss Hughes, orchestra manager, early in 1928. After discussions among Severance, Dudley Blossom (campaign chairman), and Frank H. Ginn (chairman of the building committee), McCornack was replaced by Walker and Weeks early in 1929. Ginn already had a long-standing relationship with Frank Walker through their mutual interests in Gates Mills. Throughout construction, he worked closely with the architects, meeting or corresponding with them regularly and approving all decisions, and Severance himself had a say in most major decisions, including the design of the sculptured pediment by Henry Hering above the portico. Severance Hall was constructed in 1929–30 and opened for its inaugural concert on February 5, 1931.

Elizabeth Kirk has called Severance Hall "a design in compromise,"[42] and in fact there were many functional, structural, and aesthetic priorities that had to be reconciled. Severance intended the hall to be a memorial to his wife; the auditorium had to have excellent acoustics and space for stage performances; accessibility and comfort were demanded; the university wanted it to be adaptable for lectures; and efficiency and economy had to be considered. The difficulty of the corner site was an additional challenge for the architects. Walker and Weeks's solution was a centralized polygonal building with a corner portico on a high base, approached by flights of steps and flanked by wings along the two streets. One of the most unusual features of the design was the automobile drive-through at the street level (since closed) that enabled concert goers to be deposited in the lower lobby.

The building contained the main auditorium, which seated 1,844, as well as a 400-seat chamber music hall on the ground floor and a radio broadcasting studio. On the stage there were a cyclorama and a plaster sky dome for operatic productions, although these compromised the projection of the orchestra's sound. Through the personal interest of Severance and orchestra conductor Nikolai Sokoloff, an innovative system of color lighting was developed for the auditorium and stage, operated by a clavilux or color organ console to produce innumerable changing effects. Yale Drama School professor Stanley MacCanless was the lighting consultant, and he worked closely with Walker and Weeks's electrical engineer, Dean Holden (grandson of *Plain Dealer* publisher Liberty Holden).

The classical exterior was intended to complement the Museum of Art, as well as the Allen Memorial Medical Library across the street, and its style was called Georgian upon its opening. The main entrance leads into a two-story grand foyer, elliptical in shape and daring in color, with carnelian red marble columns, gilded capitals, and bronze stylized ornamental reliefs in the art moderne style, plus decorative murals illustrating the evolution of musical instruments. These transitional stylistic features prepared the concert goer somewhat for the style of the auditorium, with its cool silver and gray reeded proscenium frame and floral filigree ceiling pattern, which were called "French modernistic" by one contemporary critic.[43] The boardroom, green room, and chamber music hall were executed in variations on the Renaissance and rococo styles, and authentic antique architectural details were incorporated in the boardroom. John L. Severance had a major part in all of these decisions. While the building may be seen as the result of a series of stylistic compromises, it is also

First Church of Christ, Scientist, interior, 1928.

a brilliant solution to a set of demanding requirements and a monument to a cultivated businessman who knew what he wanted.

Severance Hall bears more than a passing resemblance to the First Church of Christ, Scientist, originally intended for the Euclid Avenue site and finally built on the Heights overlooking University Circle. Although both buildings were erected in 1929, all of the principal features of the church were planned in 1928 and therefore prior to the design of Severance Hall. Both the neoclassical exteriors and the modernistic interiors are variations on their respective themes. If anything, the church is the more classical. The use of classicism by the Christian Science church stood for the rationalism of a faith that was believed to be based on a scientific system of reason and demonstration. The octagonal shape of

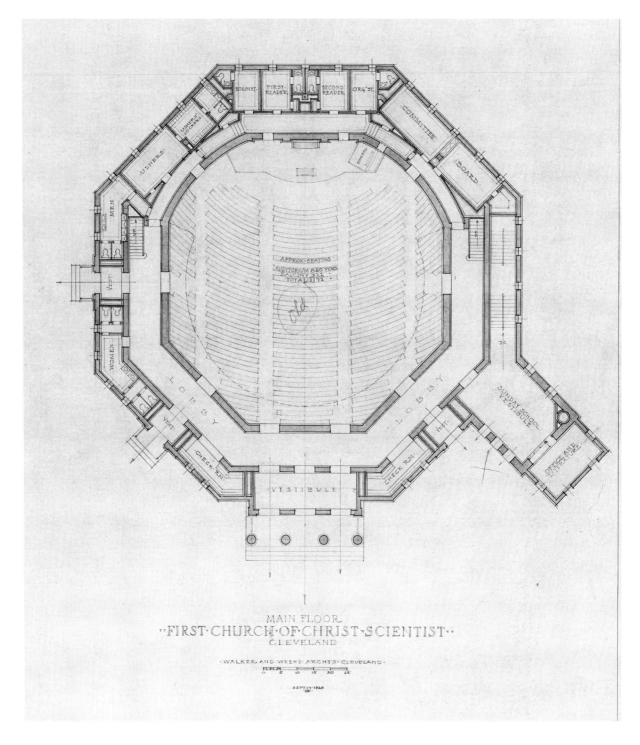

First Church of Christ, Scientist, 1928,
proposed plan.

the First Church is a clearly defined geometric solid, and the portico of four columns is a true classical temple front, instead of being elevated on an entrance podium. Indeed, the giant campanile, so untypical of Christian Science churches, becomes the chief distinguishing feature of the religious structure. The similarities between the sanctuary interior and the grand foyer of Severance Hall are even more remarkable. Although the foyer is elliptical and the church circular, both spaces are bounded by a colonnaded gallery with Ionic columns. An oculus opening to a painted sky dome in the sanctuary, a device drawn from the pagan Roman Pantheon, became a circular ceiling motif in the foyer, and the lacy filigree ornament of the church ceiling is closely echoed in the Severance Hall auditorium. One can only conclude that the designer, Dana Clark, found certain aesthetic solutions discovered in the church so satisfying as to be irresistible for reuse.

At least three institutions of higher education outside Cleveland called upon Walker and Weeks. Two of them were in Ohio, Mount Union College and Ohio Wesleyan University. Both were affiliated with the Methodist church and both had traditions going back to the 1840s. For both colleges the architects served as consultants and advisers on ambitious campus plans that were cruelly truncated by the economic disaster of the thirties. The architectural style of the proposed buildings for both campuses was Georgian colonial. While many older Eastern universities and colleges were well established in the collegiate gothic style, the colonial revival suited the aspirations, as well as the pocketbooks, of the small midwestern colleges.

At Mount Union College in Alliance, Walker and Weeks designed an "athletic auditorium" in 1921. The reason for their selection is not documented, but it is very likely that their work on the industrial housing in Alliance in 1918 brought them to the attention of the trustees of the college. The multipurpose gymnasium and assembly hall was built in 1921–22 and dedicated as Soldiers Memorial Hall, its immediate construction dictated by the enthusiasm and support of alumni. The two-story brick building had a rather barnlike interior structure with permanent U-shaped bleacher seating and a stage platform at one end. In fact, it was a smaller version of the Cleveland Public Auditorium being built at exactly the same time. The facade had Ionic columns executed in cast stone, an economical substitute for genuine masonry that became popular in the late teens. In 1928 Walker and Weeks also provided plans for concrete stadium bleachers on the athletic field seating 2,500; as it turned out, these two structures were the only projects actually constructed at Mount Union.

Some of the buildings of Greater Wesleyan
College, Macon, Georgia, 1926.

Greater Wesleyan College, Macon, Georgia,
1926, aerial view.

However, in the optimistic twenties, the college had a long-range development plan prepared that envisioned the addition of several new buildings. The college was fortunate in having a large rectangular plot on which the architects could lay out a traditional quadrangle. They had only to work around a handful of existing buildings, at the center of which was the old main, a distinguished Civil War structure in the Romanesque revival style. The administrative dean had a list of desired buildings, and Walker and Weeks prepared tentative sketches for a library, a conservatory of music, and a chapel. Different versions of the master plan were drawn, and the library was once shown with a Roman dome, like that at Columbia University's library, and once with a Georgian steeple. None of these buildings were erected, however.

For Ohio Wesleyan University in Delaware, Ohio, Walker and Weeks acted as architectural consultants for more than a decade. Unlike Mount Union, the university had a number of separate parcels that had to be linked in a meandering sort of master plan. Correspondence between Walker and university president John W. Hoffman reveals that it was necessary to write a contract to spell out what constituted consultation, what was expected of Walker and Weeks in the way of advice on plans by other architects, and what the limits were to the demands on their time. Here, too, the actual construction following Walker and Weeks's plans was little. A dormitory on which Walker and Weeks had done a great deal of preliminary planning was given to the Cleveland firm of Warner and Mitchell at the behest of Mrs. Frank Stuyvesant, the widow of the principal donor.

In 1926 Walker and Weeks also began work on the campus of Greater Wesleyan College in Macon, Georgia. Surely it is no coincidence that an influential member of the board of trustees was Colonel Sam Tate, president of the Georgia Marble Company. Under his leadership in the early 1900s, Georgia marble employed over a thousand workers, operated several quarries, and controlled a number of finishing plants. The paternalistic owner provided schools and social centers for his employees and even attempted to impose his puritanical brand of Methodism on them. He was a trustee of two other Methodist colleges in addition to Wesleyan College. More important, Tate was an enthusiastic advocate of marble for public edifices; he is said to have influenced the selection of the stone for the statue of Abraham Lincoln in the Lincoln Memorial. Needless to say, Walker and Weeks's prominent role in the design of banking, commercial, and office buildings in the Midwest made their clients among Tate's best customers. In 1924 Tate had them design a home for himself in the small family town of Tate in Pickens County, Georgia. It was constructed entirely of marble, including the garage, with an interior structure of iron and concrete.

For Wesleyan College Walker and Weeks prepared a master plan including academic and administration buildings, a chapel, a gymnasium, and a dormitory quadrangle. The design of the buildings is an austere Georgian colonial style of red brick and white trim, like the Ohio colleges. The buildings, simple rectangular two- and three-story blocks with gabled roofs, are adorned with classical columns and Palladian windows, but the detail is executed not in wood but in marble. The result is that the architectural elements are more crisp and attenuated than they would otherwise have been. This in turn gives the proportions of the buildings a spare and fragile appearance that is uncommon in the Georgian idiom. Ultimately, these considerations demonstrate the impact on an architectural design of two disparate constraints, the nature of materials, and an autocratic decision making.

Walker and Weeks also created campuses for two private preparatory schools in Shaker Heights between 1924 and 1926. The campuses are totally different in spite of their kindred programs. University School for boys and Hathaway Brown School for girls both needed classrooms for primary, middle, and upper schools, as well as offices, a library, a principal's office, dormitories, an assembly hall, and gymnasiums and athletic fields. The only major difference was University School's need for manual training shops to carry out the school's aim of combining practical skills with academic schooling. Both plans were first developed in 1924, but University School undertook an aggressive fund-raising campaign and was able to build in 1925. It was not until 1926, when, to attract it to Shaker Heights, the Van Sweringens offered Hathaway Brown a tract of land, that the girls' school was able to proceed.

With so many things being equal, it is difficult to account for the astonishing difference in the visual impact of the finished buildings. There are almost no references in any of Walker and Weeks's existing office records to explain their choice of a particular style. There seems to be no documentation for the choice of the Georgian for University School; but as an American colonial style, it expressed the school's goal of developing good citizens. The central tower recalls both the New England meetinghouse and a government building like Independence Hall. The proportions of the tower and belfry are correct according to that tradition, but because the administration building behind the tower is so stunted in size, the tower appears abnormally tall and slender by contrast. Likewise, the flanking buildings for dormitories and classrooms, in their red brick and marble trim, are a competent exercise in Georgian public building, but the one-story, flat-roofed connecting wings are so utilitarian looking and unrelated to the three main buildings that the ensemble has a disjointed effect.

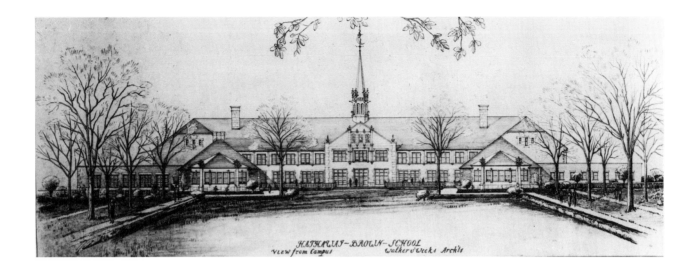

HATHAWAY-BROWN-SCHOOL
View from Campus   Walker & Weeks Archts

Hathaway Brown School, Shaker
Heights, 1926.

A clue to the design of Hathaway Brown School is found in a letter from Frank Walker to the school's head, Mary E. Raymond, in which he notes his understanding that "the general type of the building should be as rambling as possible consistent with reasonable economy."[44] The grouping of all of the functions in one large U-shaped building, with only the dormitory separate, created a much more coherent scheme than the boys' school group. "Rambling" also suggests a desire to create an effect appropriate to the suburban residential neighborhood. A year later an elevation was submitted to the building committee showing the "type of architecture" proposed. It is possible that the Tudor style was chosen partly as a reminiscence of the twenty-year-old stone Hathaway Brown building in Cleveland, which Walker and Weeks had made measured drawings of when beginning on the new plans. If University School's rendering of the Georgian and Hathaway Brown's Tudor style are compared, and in spite of today's strictures against gender-linked stereotypes, terms like "Spartan" for the boys' school and "homey" for the girls' school come irresistibly to mind. In those terms, as well as the visual coherence of the respective groups, Hathaway Brown is unquestionably the more successful.

The churches of Walker and Weeks reveal as much variety as their other buildings, the most magnificent being the Euclid Avenue Baptist Church. The church decided to undertake a most ambitious project in 1921 when it took an option on property on the northwest corner of Euclid Avenue and East 18th Street, worth $1,325,000, and the plans called for a building costing more than $1 million. The corner itself was occupied by a commercial building that would provide revenue, and the church was built behind it facing the side street. The preliminary program and sketches were developed beginning in November 1921. Harry Weeks was

Euclid Avenue Baptist Church, 1924, as
designed.

a member of the board of trustees, and he prepared a description of the building program and the design, reporting, "I believe as much time was spent in preliminary study as for any building I have been connected with."[45] The new chapel of the church was erected in 1925–26. Continued work was only made possible by contributions of $200,000 from John D. Rockefeller and $50,000 from John D. Rockefeller Jr., in addition to which John D. Jr. bought the old church property for $800,000, making it possible to go ahead with construction. In the summer of 1926 he inspected the building with Weeks to see what his contributions had accomplished.

The ambitious plant, completed in 1927, contained a chapel seating 645 people, a main auditorium with a capacity of 2,200, a basement banquet hall seating 1,000, two additional dining rooms for 250 persons, offices, and a Sunday school that would ultimately serve 3,000 pupils. The tower was designed to reach the height of 175 feet and to give access to seven stories of classrooms. Only two stories of the Sunday school building were completed, however, and the tower was never finished.

Weeks later quoted a published description of the architecture by Romer Shawhan, A.I.A.: "It seems to have remained for a Cleveland firm of architects to employ, in the Euclid Avenue Baptist Church, the first 'all polychrome terra cotta' design in this country. As far as known by the writer, it is the most elaborate attempt ever made in the use of polychrome terra cotta in architecture." Shawhan described the style as an adaptation of the Lombard Romanesque style, which inspired the use of brick. Weeks said that "after considerable research and investigation of available materials, the architects decided to made the church an all-ceramic building. Special bricks of terra cotta were made by the same manufacturer who furnished the polychrome ornament for the exterior."[46] The walls of the church were executed in brown terra-cotta and the ornament accented in brilliantly colored glazed terra-cotta.

The iconographic scheme was integral with the design and material. J. Byers Hays wrote, "The whole fabric of the church, its plan and many details, are capable of expressing religious truth in a symbolic language of its own. . . . The very building itself thus becomes a Bible for all."[47] The main entrance archway contained a terra-cotta screen with symbols of the early history of the church and was flanked by heroic polychrome figures of John the Baptist and Roger Williams. The symbolism was carried into the interior of the main auditorium, especially in the coffered ceiling of the chapel, which had symbols etched in plastic paint in the manner of antique sgraffito. Sadly, the membership of the church declined beginning in the mid-thirties, and this masterpiece of architecture and art was lost: the church closed in 1956, and the building was torn down in 1961.

St. Paul's Episcopal Church, Cleveland
Heights, 1928.

St. Paul's Episcopal Church, under construction, 1928.

Walker and Weeks were also responsible for two of the most typical suburban churches in the gothic style—the First Baptist Church and St. Paul's Episcopal Church. St. Paul's moved from its Euclid Avenue building of 1876 to Cleveland Heights, where its parish hall was erected in 1927–28. The 150-foot gothic bell tower was added in 1929, but the depression prevented the completion of the original plan. Partner J. Byers Hays was the designer, and after he left Walker and Weeks in 1930, he finished St. Paul's independently. The chapel and the walls of the main sanctuary were built in 1941, but rising wartime costs made it impossible to continue. In 1947 Hays proposed a revised scheme for the nave, with a lower, flat ceiling instead of the high vaulting, and the sanctuary was erected in 1949–51. Most observers consider the original parish hall and tower the most successful portions of St. Paul's; as serious as the compromises to the original concept were, they are testimony to the talent and inventiveness of Hays.

First Baptist Church, Shaker Heights, 1928.

The First Baptist Church completed its new building in 1928–29 after moving from downtown Cleveland to Shaker Heights. Ambrose Swasey was chairman of the architectural design committee, and W. H. Prescott, for whom Walker and Weeks had designed a residence in 1915, was the finance committee chairman. Because of the desirability of situating the church on a prominent location set off by three residential boulevards, the Van Sweringen Company sold an eight-acre parcel to the church for less than half its estimated value. The company reserved the right of design approval, and in 1927, when working drawings were already being prepared, the Van Sweringen's vice president expressed concern that the rear elevation of the church facing Shelburne Road should have the proper character. Prescott reassured the company, and the three-dimensional treatment of the entire group succeeds in giving the impression of an English cathedral close. First Baptist is like the Euclid Avenue Baptist Church in its extensive use of biblical symbolism and in the large church-school plant. The school rooms, assembly hall, parlor, and office are arranged around an interior court 75 by 120 feet, much like a cloister.

Since the church was completed in one building program, it is much more consistent throughout than St. Paul's and probably gives a good impression of how that church would have looked if the original scheme had been carried out. Also designed by Hays in a similar gothic style, First Baptist shows more of the simplification seen in other buildings of the late twenties. The beautifully geometric 130-foot tower was reportedly approved by Swasey only after a number of other sketches were rejected, even though it cost $50,000 more. The 65-foot ceiling of the sanctuary is roofed by simple triangular oak trusses, not by vaulting. The aisle piers are plain octagonal shafts with none of the clustered vertical moldings that a strictly historical gothic treatment would dictate. As with most revivalist work of the period, the ultimate aim was not to create a historical replica but to provide sufficient style reference to convey a convincing sense of the meaning of the building.

This cavalcade of buildings for churches, hospitals, universities, libraries, and schools prompts some reflection on the nature of architectural expression. It may be said that all of these purposes—the conservation and dissemination of knowledge, the care of the less fortunate, artistic and musical expression, religious worship and practice—are part of the quest for the values of the ideal life. All of the buildings attempted in some way or another to embody those values. It so happened that they were built in a period when historical style was understood as an expression of content. The architects of Walker and Weeks's generation firmly believed that a permanent expressive value had been embodied in the styles and forms of certain ages. It was not only in the superficial sense (a Roman bank for security and integrity, a gothic church for religious faith); it was rather that certain forms had been discovered that were good for all time, and certain intrinsic values and meanings were attached to those forms. Not inconsistently, the architects saw that twentieth-century America might be on the road to developing a style that would express the values of its own age.

Moreover, these buildings were created with the explicit purpose of being classic—not in the narrow sense of being based on antique architecture, but of adhering to established standards and having lasting value. That purpose has been borne out by time; these institutional buildings look as permanent and as right seventy years after they were erected as they did when new. Furthermore, they do it better than many younger buildings avowedly designed to be "relevant" to their times. Although clearly of the date when they were built, these buildings have not become "dated."

chapter 7

ENGINEERING CONSULTANTS

From the late teens to the end of the thirties, Walker and Weeks were connected with the design of a number of engineering works, principally bridges, in which collaboration between architect and engineer was undertaken in varying degrees. We know that Walker and Weeks's office had its own engineering staff in addition to its planners and designers. Moreover, it goes without saying that the mastery of engineering is fundamental to the stability of architecture. But the relationship between architectural and engineering design is neither unvarying nor simple. The traditional view of early-twentieth-century criticism is that a deep dichotomy existed between structure and aesthetics, especially in the work of the beaux-arts-trained architects. In this view the only redeeming aspect of the period was the work of Louis Sullivan, and his formulation of the dictum "form follows function," and certain experiments in the expression of structural forms by Frank Lloyd Wright, Walter Gropius, Mies van der Rohe, and others. Less attention has been given to the serious attempts by academic architects to integrate architectural design and utilitarian engineering. Such efforts were widespread, even though they often consisted of the embellishment of engineering with ornament, in spite of declarations of intent to the contrary. Gustav Lindenthal, New York engineer and designer of the Hell Gate Bridge, stated the case succinctly in an address before the Cleveland Engineering Society in 1916: "Since the building architect does not include in his work the construction of bridges, and on the other hand, the bridge engineer usually does not include in his studies the contemplation of pleasing forms, it should be the rule for any important, truly monumental bridge structure, that engineer and architect work together."[48]

Apart from several small ornamental stone bridges built on suburban estates like those of Hanna and White in the teens, Walker and Weeks's first major bridge design was the result of another war memorial competition in 1927, and it was probably the purest in architectural form. Three memorials were to be erected in Europe to commemorate the action of the 37th Division in the First World War. The competition was held by

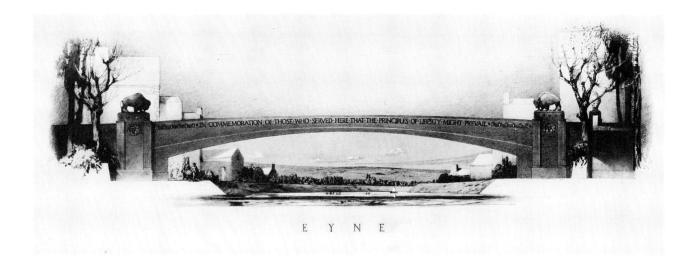

E Y N E

Thirty-seventh Division Memorial Bridge,
near Eyne, Belgium, 1927.

the 37th Division Battle Monument Commission of Ohio, and the jury—
consisting of Paul Cret, Philip Goodwin (architect of the Museum of
Modern Art in 1939), and Benjamin Morris—selected Walker and Weeks
for the bridge in Belgium. Walker and Weeks submitted designs for the
other two memorials, at Montfaucon and Hattonchatel, France, but did
not place in either competition. No doubt they were encouraged to enter
the competition for all three because of their success with the Indiana
World War Memorial. Laurence H. Norton, who had served with the
division, was the secretary of the 37th Division commission and the principal contact with the architects. Norton was an executive in Cleveland's
Oglebay-Norton mining and shipping company and was secretary to
Myron T. Herrick, U.S. ambassador to France, in 1919.

Belgian workers constructed the bridge in 1928–29. It crosses the river
Scheldt (l'Escaut) near Eyne, twenty kilometers south of Ghent, where
the division attacked and advanced on the German forces in the last days
of the war in November 1918. Armen Tashjian went to Belgium at the
expense of the monument commission to supervise the construction. The
slenderness of the reinforced concrete arch, which spans the river in a
simple graceful curve, is closer in spirit to that of the contemporary European bridges of Freyssinet and Maillart, which are far slimmer and more
daring than most of their American counterparts. The abutments at ether
end of the bridge carry concrete statues of the native American bison.

In the realm of the completely utilitarian bridge, Walker and Weeks
consulted in 1929 on the design of four railway viaducts for the New York
Central and Nickel Plate Railroads. Familiar to hundreds of Cleveland
commuters daily at the approaches to the Heights, the heavy steel girder
bridges cross Euclid Avenue, Mayfield Road, Cedar Glen, and East

Boulevard. The abutments have deeply fluted piers in the plain geometric lines of the modernistic style, and the concrete wing walls are rusticated as if built of stone. In fact, they were originally planned to be in stone, but with the substitution of concrete the difference in the nature of the materials was not expressed, and the masonry elements seem to have little relationship to the steel plate girders they support. It is possible that the architectural reconciliation of steel and concrete forms was inherently insoluble in the idioms of the period. Alternate designs showed additional ornament on the metal supports and railings, but it is not likely that they would have solved the problem either.

Frank Walker's further involvement in bridge design might not have come about if it were not for Wilbur J. Watson, a Cleveland engineer who was in the forefront of early concrete bridge design. Watson was among the first twentieth-century civil engineers to espouse the cause of a genuine partnership between science and art, and he was one of the most articulate proponents of the collaboration between engineer and architect. He wrote several books in the twenties and thirties in which he stated his views. He summarized his basic premise as follows:

> It is highly desirable that utilitarian structures such as bridges should be as pleasing to the eye as it is practicable to make them, and that there should be greater collaboration between the architect and the engineer, with the realization on the part of each that science without art is apt to be unattractive and art without science inefficient.... There is considerable difference among writers on many questions of architectural design, such as the propriety of using the classical architectural motives as ornamental features on bridges.[49]

Watson insisted that the architect's contribution should not be understood merely as adding ornament to an already-engineered structure. Often the engineer has more than one solution available that answers a construction problem, but he has no particular criteria for the final choice. The architect's training in design and his sensitivity to relationships of form and materials enable him to select and define the forms that will be the most significant and expressive.

The first major collaboration between Watson and Walker was the Lorain-Carnegie Bridge in Cleveland, planned and erected in 1928–30. A high-level bridge crossing the Cuyahoga Valley at Lorain Avenue had been envisioned at least as early as 1911. In 1925 a special committee of the City Plan Commission recommended that the bridge should be built immediately, and an $8 million bond issue was passed in 1927. The concrete and steel structure, nearly a mile long, consists of thirteen cantilever spans varying in length from 299 feet over the river to 132 feet at the ends. With reference to this bridge, Watson noted that

Lorain-Carnegie (Central-Lorain) Bridge
pylons, 1929.

Great care was taken to obtain a pleasing architectural creation, demanded by a public that is becoming more and more critical in this regard. This is a manifestation that modern civilization is not satisfied with structures of utility alone, but desires that art shall be considered. As a result of this insistence of a more enlightened civilization, there is an increasing tendency for collaboration between engineers and architects in the design of the more important bridges.[50]

The features of the bridge subject to architectural consideration were the curved lower chords of the steel trusses, the concrete facing wall carrying the piers up to the roadway, the pedestals between trusses, the stone and aluminum railings, and the sculptured pylons. The most significant of these are the four massive pylons with carved figures of "Guardians of Traffic." Designed by Walker and sculptured by Henry Hering, they represent the simplified classicism that was becoming modernistic in sculpture as well as architecture. The figures hold in their hands vehicles representing the spirit of progress in transportation: a hay rack, a covered wagon, a stage coach, a passenger automobile, and four types of motor trucks. The Lorain-Carnegie sculptures are rare among bridge pylons designed during those years because of the integral character of the figures and the pylons, the appropriateness of the symbolism, the consistency of the style, and the scale of the figures. The guardian figures still convey an imaginative power of a kind that has almost become lost in an increasingly technological society.

A lower bridge deck intended to carry four lanes of vehicular traffic and two streetcar tracks was never completed because of the lack of financing. Even before this became evident, there was opposition to the extra traffic lanes because of the complicated approaches at the eastern end of the bridge. Four major streets—Ontario, Central (Carnegie), Woodland, and Broadway—came together at the east end of the bridge. The solution proposed was a 500-foot traffic circle with a park in the center. An even more extravagant beaux-arts fantasy was drawn for the western approach to the bridge. An open plaza that would have encompassed all of the existing Market Square district was framed with symmetrical buildings on a grand scale, like the baroque squares of Europe. Walker and Weeks's brilliant beaux-arts plans with radiating streets had all the grandeur of the boulevards of L'Enfant in Washington or Haussmann in Paris.

In 1930 Wilbur Watson was appointed consulting engineer for the proposed Main Avenue Bridge, another high-level bridge over the Cuyahoga River, with Walker as consulting architect. Walker and Weeks carried out a great deal of preliminary design work in 1931–32, including an unexpected amount of planning for the approaches connecting the bridge with

Forest Hills Pedestrian Bridge, East Cleveland, 1939.

Bulkley Boulevard on the west side and West 3d Street on the east. The proposed bridge consisted of multiple arched spans, and Walker developed plans for the stone piers and a traffic control station at the western end. Because of the depression, the county commissioners halted the planning in 1932. When it was resumed in 1938 and the existing Main Avenue Viaduct was constructed, Walker was no longer included. It is one of the footnotes on the depression that Walker and Weeks's account for the work undertaken through 1932 was not fully paid until 1939.

In 1939 Watson again sought Walker's collaboration on three projects. The first was an ornamental pedestrian bridge over Forest Hill Boulevard in East Cleveland on the original estate of John D. Rockefeller. Faced with a warm yellow Berea sandstone, it is actually a reinforced-concrete arch that springs 140 feet across the roadway. The stone is ornamented with large circular medallions at either end. Albert D. Taylor, the landscape architect who worked with Walker and Weeks on residential commissions and other occasions, was the landscaping consultant.

Two remaining bridges designed by Watson as engineer and Walker as consulting architect were erected in Lorain, Ohio, in 1939–40. The first was the Erie Street Bridge over the Black River, a 339-foot-long, double-leaf bascule bridge that was described at the time as the longest such bridge in the world. Among the parts requiring Walker's architectural treatment were two lookout towers for the bridge operators, ornamental stone benches sculptured into an approach parapet at the eastern end, and inscribed markers giving the data of the bridge's construction. The second Lorain bridge was the Central High-Level, a cantilever structure over the Black River at 21st Street. For the approaches Walker planned pairs of forty-foot stone pylons with a stepped modernistic profile, not unlike those on the Lorain-Carnegie Bridge in Cleveland, except that these were completely abstract and without sculptured figures. However, work on this PWA-subsidized project was cut back because of the economic conditions, and the pylons were never executed.

If Frank Walker's personal interest in design lay primarily with residences, his other most frequent involvement was in engineering consultation. Two different forces were at work in the subtle balance between design and engineering in the works of this period. One was the tendency to see the architect's role as ornamental, which, in spite of Watson's protestation to the contrary, was all too often the result—and, in all fairness, it should be said that Walker's contribution often erred on the side of ornamentation. The other was the understanding that the frank revelation of structure could create a beauty of its own. This positive point of view was recognized by engineers, industrial designers, and modern architects alike among Walker's contemporaries. (It should be remembered that Walker was eight years younger than Frank Lloyd Wright.) It is now abundantly clear that the complete triumph of functionalism did not guarantee good design, and by the late 1930s there were already perceptive critics who recognized the danger of the functionalist principle developing into a new academicism.

Walker's association with Watson came at a brief moment in history whose promise was destined not to be fulfilled. The situation since the days of Watson and Walker is not unlike that described by Lindenthal in 1916: "It is regrettable that many large bridge structures in or near cities have been built without sufficient regard for appearance and usually with the excuse that aesthetics cost money and are, therefore, an unnecessary expense. This is not true in most cases. It is merely the lack of study and skill in the designer, which is not creditable to the noble profession of engineering."[51] A more plausible reason for the disappearance of Watson's "critical public," if it ever existed, was the breakdown of any consensus on design principles. It was the engineers and architects themselves who had that vision.

chapter 8

1935 AND AFTER

Harry E. Weeks died on December 21, 1935, at the age of sixty-four. He had been active in the firm until two years earlier, when ill health forced him to spend much of his time away from Cleveland. The funeral was held at his home at 2357 Tudor Drive in Cleveland Heights, which the firm had remodeled for him eight years before (it was the former residence of manufacturer John C. Lowe). Weeks's death ended thirty years of association with Frank Walker. Although he did not enjoy Walker's renown and general popularity, Weeks was the organizer and officer manager, and the best evidence suggests that he was behind the basic organization responsible for the firm's success as an "architectural factory." After his death, the firm continued under the name of Walker and Weeks for another fourteen years, with Walker at the helm, and some of its most impressive and important commissions were built during the period.

Like every business, the practice of architecture in the thirties was depressed because of the general economic conditions in the country. The extent of the calamity has been thoroughly documented; among the most telling statistics are the facts that industrial production in 1932 was less than one-half the 1929 volume, and the total wages paid were 60 percent less than in 1929. Many men had to be laid off. Walker and Weeks's office records are full of correspondence pleading for payment on accounts; in many cases, like the Main Avenue Bridge work, settlement was made years later, if ever. The capture of a few large commissions, like the Cleveland Post Office, no doubt saved the office from shutting down completely.

Another federal government job was the architectural consultation on a series of locks and dams on the Ohio and Kanawha Rivers in 1933–34. One of the most remarkable of the PWA-funded engineering projects of the decade, it comprised the Gallipolis Locks and Dam on the Ohio, about fourteen miles below the mouth of the Kanawha River, and three dams on the Kanawha at Marmet, London, and Winfield in West Virginia. The Gallipolis dam at that time was the largest roller dam in the world. It has eight concrete piers 135 feet in height spaced at 125-foot intervals across the river. The piers support steel rollers that control the water level as they are mechanically raised or lowered. Thus the dam regulates the mean water level for forty-eight miles above it on the Ohio

Kanawha River Locks and Dam, West Virginia, 1933–34.

and for thirty-five miles up the Kanawha. The two locks at the West Virginia end of the Gallipolis dam are 110 feet wide and allow the passage of the largest barges. The Marmet and London dams were completed in 1934, the Winfield dam in 1937, and the Gallipolis Locks and Dam in 1938 at a cost of $10.4 million. Frank Walker included his consultation on the project among the important commissions in his authorized biography and in his job resume when applying for other government commissions.

A great many jobs during the depression years consisted of the remodeling or alteration of existing structures. And here old friendships helped. Considerable work was done on Frank H. Ginn's home in Gates Mills in 1933, and his law firm, Tolles, Hogsett, Ginn & Morley, had Walker and Weeks renovate their offices in the Union Commerce Building in 1937. A Winton Motor Car showroom building built in 1905 on Huron Road in Cleveland was renovated for Engel and Fetzer's fur store in 1936 with storage vaults and a mezzanine. For Rosenblum's clothing store, a two-story building on Euclid Avenue that also housed the popular Mills Restaurant, Walker and Weeks added a third story in 1939. They redesigned

The Arcade, alterations, 1939
(Martin Linsey).

the interiors of Cleveland's Statler Hotel in 1937, creating a new lobby and dining room. Among the commissions outside of Cleveland, Walker and Weeks renovated banks in Evansville, Indiana, and in Pittsburgh and the Toledo Trust Company and D. H. Burnham's Ford Building in Detroit. But the most notorious example of their renovation work was the alteration of the Euclid Avenue facade of the world-famous Cleveland Arcade in 1939. The great stone Richardsonian arched portal was removed and replaced with a square entrance, and steel beams were inserted to support the masonry tower. The first two stories were faced with polished granite, and the entrance was adorned with relief medallions of the profiles of Stephen Harkness and Charles Brush, the original president and vice president of the Arcade Company.

Court of the Presidents, Great Lakes
Exposition, 1935–36.

By 1935 sufficient optimism had been regained that the business community began making preparations for the Great Lakes Exposition in Cleveland, planned to celebrate the industrial empire of the eight states bordering on the Great Lakes. In addition, the year 1936 was the centennial of Cleveland's incorporation as a city. The exposition was not called a world's fair, and it was smaller in scope than the better-known fairs of the thirties in Chicago and New York. The design was entirely in the hands of local architects, but they benefited from the experience of Albert N. Gonsior, who was in charge of construction at the Chicago Century of Progress in 1933, where much experimental work with quick and inexpensive construction was done. Walker was appointed to the seven-member committee on architecture for the exposition. Abram Garfield was chairman, and Walker's former colleague Byers Hays was also a member. Another former co-worker, Byron Hunsicker, was supervising architect of the Streets of the World, the international village and entertainment area. The three major exhibition buildings were awarded to Antonio diNardo, Hays & Simpson, and Warner & Mitchell. The architects described the style of the exposition buildings as "simple, straight-forward, colorful and severe" and expressed the hope that they would "establish a trend in modern design just as did the buildings of the Columbian Exposition and the Century of Progress."[52] Land on the shore of Lake Erie was filled and graded, buildings were erected, and landscaping was completed for the opening on June 28, 1936.

The entrance plaza of the Great Lakes Exposition occupied the central part of the Mall. Walker and Weeks were assigned the Court of the Presidents, a pedestrian and vehicular bridge over the railroad tracks to connect the Mall with the lakefront exhibition area below. The bridge, 100 feet wide and 350 feet long, honored the sixteen U.S. presidents who were either natives of or elected from Ohio. It was lined with some sixty shops and concession booths and carried fourteen gilded sculptured eagles executed in the stylized classicism of the thirties. Walker and Weeks also planned the pedestrian underpass beneath East 9th Street that connected the main exposition grounds near the stadium with the midway amusement area to the east. The firm drew plans for a casino for the Leisy brewery, a fanciful wooden building of three linked octagonal pagodalike structures, but the records suggest that it was not built. Walker also designed a temple pavilion with a stone grotto and ornamental iron fencing for the model garden of the Gates Mills Garden Club, of which Mrs. Walker was a member.

The Great Lakes Exposition did not exactly "establish a trend in modern design" as the architects had hoped, but the mood of experimentation, both in forms and materials, was in the air. In the same year of 1936,

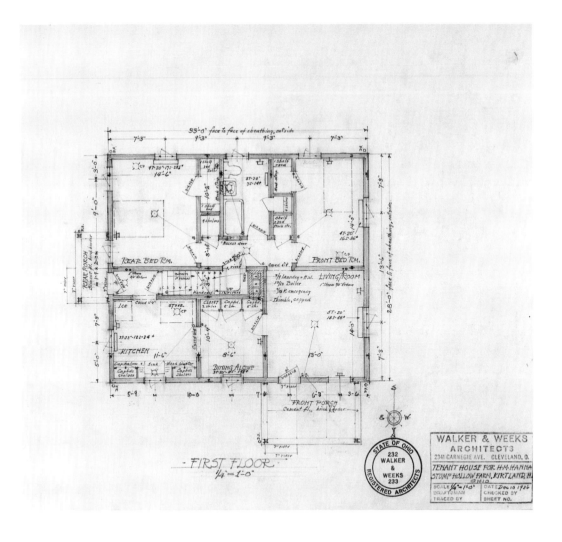

H. M. Hanna Tenant House, Kirtland, 1936.

Walker and Weeks made an unusual addition to the extensive farm complex that they began more than a dozen years before for Howard M. Hanna Jr. in Kirtland Hills, east of Cleveland. The owner of Stump Hollow Farm was a nephew of Marcus Hanna and chairman of the M. A. Hanna Company. The new building was a small tenant house in a vernacular Greek revival idiom, but its studs, rafters, and window frames were made of steel and fabricated by Stran Steel Corporation. This was only one of a number of experimental steel houses of the thirties; one of the first was designed by Philip Small's partner Charles Bacon Rowley in 1932. A steel frame, sheet steel walls, and porcelain enamel exterior shingles had all been tried. In this case, the concealing of the steel frame beneath a historical cloak, in order to harmonize with the rest of the Hanna farm buildings, simply indicates that the technology was a means to an end, and not an end in itself.

One of the designs for the Dairyland Store, 1940. The actual structure was quite different.

Walker's reputation extended as far away as Florida. In 1939–40 he was the adviser and consultant in charge of planning the harbor and a new city at Port Canaveral. The bird's-eye-view drawing from the Walker and Weeks office shows the ship channel that cuts through the cape, a railroad trestle and causeway across the Banana River, Merritt Island and Indian River, a foreign trade zone, oil tanks and wharves, a yacht basin, and a commercial seaplane base. The layout of the new city was indicated to the north of the port on the cape that was acquired by the U.S. Air Force in 1949 for a missile proving ground. Little of Walker's plan was carried out; the intensive development of the port began under the Canaveral Port Authority in the 1950s, and the city of Cape Canaveral grew up south of the port a decade later, achieving a population of 4,500 by 1970.

The most unlikely work to come from the same office that produced the Indiana World War Memorial may have been a little neighborhood convenience store hidden on East 65th Street in Cleveland just around the corner from its parent, the Meyer Dairy. Walker and Weeks's Dairyland Store, built in 1940, was a quintessential roadside artifact. Large expanses of window opened into the sales area, and a flat, projecting canopy anticipated the fifties' diner-cum-drive-in. Most startling of all was a milk bottle some ten feet tall standing on the roof, an icon in the tradition of the hot dogs, giant barbecue pigs, and brown derbies of the period, later to be enshrined in pop art.

Frank Walker remained active throughout the forties, and at the age of sixty-five he was invited in the spring of 1942 to be one of three jurors for a design competition for the campus at Wayne University in Detroit. The other two jurors were Joseph Hudnut, dean of the Harvard School of Design, and Walter R. McCornack, former Cleveland architect and dean of the School of Architecture at the Massachusetts Institute of Technology. The prospectus was twofold: a design for a student center building and a grouping plan for a three-block-long campus comprising eight new buildings. The professional adviser for the competition was Branson Gamber of Detroit's Derrick and Gamber, architects of the Henry Ford Museum at Greenfield Village. Of forty-six original entrants, many withdrew because of the pressure of wartime work, and only eleven final entries were received. The jury awarded first place to Suren Pilafian, a thirty-two-year-old Armenian-born architect. More interesting is the fact that second place went to Saarinen and Swanson, in which Eliel Saarinen was still active with his daughter Pipsan, son Eero, and Eero's wife, Lily Swann. The jury found the Saarinen entry to have "a certain distinction and poetic quality" but also "a certain lack of practical judgment,"[53] chiefly because it incorporated a tall tower that did not fit the university's programmatic requirements as well as Pilafian's plan. The Board of Education (Wayne was then a municipal university administered by the school board) accepted the jury's decision, and much of Pilafian's plan was carried out in the late forties and early fifties.

The wartime years in general, however, brought as many false starts and aborted commissions as the depression years, though there were still small residential commissions and numerous commercial remodeling jobs. A great deal of correspondence in 1940–44 was devoted to applying to governmental agencies for defense work, such as the housing project at the Ravenna (Ohio) Arsenal, the U.S. War Department, the Navy's Bureau of Yards and Docks, and the Ohio Welfare Department, as well as various influential government officials. Beginning in 1944 Walker was consultant to Eggers and Higgins of Washington, D.C., on the Army Medical Library that was being planned as part of the Library of Congress group. However, the facility was built instead in Bethesda, Maryland, after the war. Walker and Weeks drew up complete site plans in 1942 for a Defense Housing Project for the Cleveland Metropolitan Housing Authority in Bedford, Ohio, southeast of Cleveland, but the project was canceled. The proposed site consisted of seventy-five acres in the northern part of the city, and the project comprised 160 residential units of several types, including one- and two-bedroom houses, two-story row houses, an administration building, and a community building, all planned in frame, brick, and concrete block construction.

By the postwar period, the new style that had been innovative a decade before, with its streamlined expanses of wall, lack of historical ornament, flat roofs, horizontal bands of windows, and frank use of new materials,

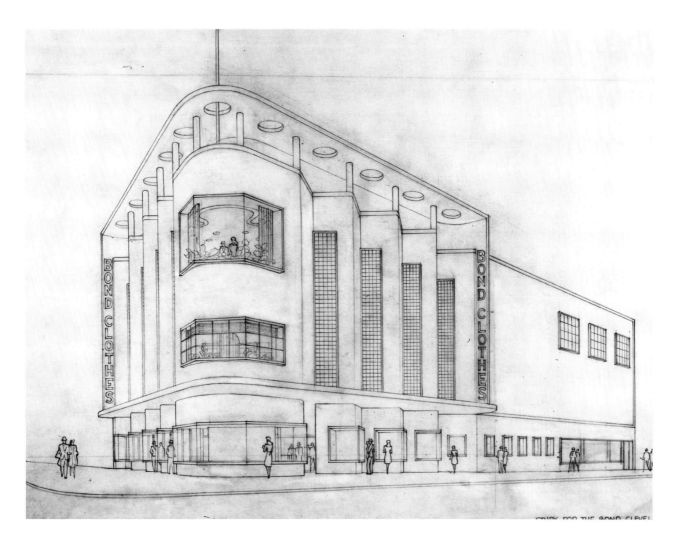

One of the designs, very similar to what was
actually built, for the Bond Store, 1945.

was a commonplace manner for retail commerce. With the Bond Store, built in 1945–47, Walker and Weeks designed the most remarkable example of streamlined modernism in Cleveland. The owners of the nineteenth-century Hickox Building on the corner of Euclid and East 9th Street decided to replace it with a new building and contracted with Bond's clothing stores of New York as tenant in May 1944. Three architects prepared plans, and Walker and Weeks were selected as the local architects. The interior layout of the sales floors and their fixtures was made by Herbert B. Beidler, a former Clevelander then practicing in Chicago. His floor plan was essentially ready by the end of 1944, and Bond's had settled on a three-story building with a well-hole through the floors "to effect the appearance of a mezzanine."[54]

Walker and Weeks worked simultaneously on plans for the exteriors. An unequal amount of documentation survives for these plans, including more than three hundred sketches and drawings of at least six different versions. An early drawing for the Hickox Building Company, even predating the Bond Store agreement, depicts a twelve-story building that is essentially the old Hickox Building clad in banks of windows in the international style. The Bond store began as a plain, windowless, rectangular box that was quickly transformed into a windowed Bauhaus-like block with a square sign pylon. But the acute angle of the corner, plus the fact that the basement walls and certain column footings of the Hickox Building would be retained, brought the design back to a curved corner bay. The first of these ideas, with a tall vertical pylon, closely resembled the Greyhound Bus Terminal that was about to be built to W. S. Arrasmith's design not far away on Chester Avenue. A related scheme had two pylons on the curve, much like a world's fair pavilion of the thirties. All of these were rejected by Bond's, until in January 1945 the final scheme was drawn by Elmer Babb in Walker and Weeks's office. Construction was halted by wartime restrictions still in effect. However, because of the reuse of the foundations, the building was defined as the rebuilding of an existing structure and construction was allowed to proceed in November 1945. It is worth noting that while Howard F. Horn was the office manager and Elmer Babb was in charge of the project, Frank Walker was still very active and took part in the client conferences in Bond's New York office.

In the final design, the cylindrical corner bay was topped by a hovering roof canopy pierced with circular holes and illuminated by spotlights. At the third-floor level a curved solarium and display area projected from the corner. A sawtooth plan on the side elevations made angled show windows so that shoppers were taken out of the sidewalk traffic. The use of solid permanent materials–pink granite and plaid terra-cotta, steel and aluminum–balanced these theatrical aspects. Remarkable as the exterior

General Plan, Case School of Applied
Science, 1944.

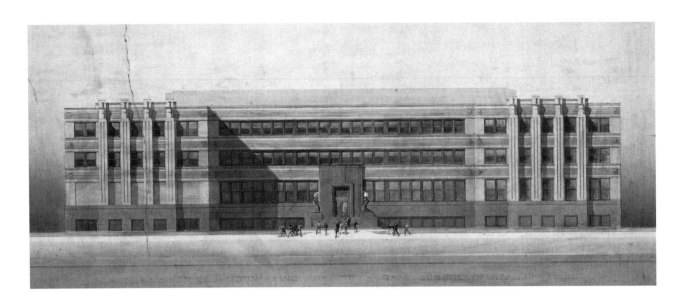

Chemical Engineering Building, Case School, 1938.

was, the spectacular interior evoked even more the spirit of the world's fairs and film musicals of the thirties. A long well opened from the main floor to the second, and a smaller circular one from the second to the third. Illuminated mirrored columns extended from the main floor through both wells to the third floor, and curved and "floating" stairways soared to the upper floors. On the third floor the wall of the sales area was a continuous undulating curve, and the total effect was one of the most baroque spaces in the city. All of the interiors were trimmed with aluminum, finished natural, satin, or black. There was indirect lighting in several colors, and fifty-two pastel shades were used in the interior decoration. Fluorescent lighting was controlled in varying degrees of intensity and enhanced by spotlights. The storefront show windows were lighted through louvered ceilings. As a dramatic and consistently designed setting for the retail sales function, Walker and Weeks's Bond Store represented the climax of the thirties' brand of modernism in Cleveland.

It was to be expected that the institutional application of the modern style was less flamboyant. In 1944 Walker and Weeks prepared a campus plan for the Case School of Applied Science at University Circle. They had already designed a distinguished modernistic building for chemical engineering at the Case School in 1939. Unlike the strong three-dimensionality of a building like the Bond Store, the architectural character of the Chemical Engineering Building is limited to the facades. The two visible elevations are defined by strong horizontal ribbons of brick, and although the original plan included prominent end wings with strong vertical piers, only the middle third of the plan was built. The center entrance is framed by a large red-granite panel (not unlike the altered

Tomlinson Hall, Case School, 1945.

Arcade entrance), a bronze allegorical figure stands above the doorway, and streamlined bronze stair railings complete the modern look. The building has since suffered additional compromise from overcrowding by other campus buildings, but it remains a pleasant reminder of a more cultivated aspect of thirties modernism.

Not surprisingly, the 1944 campus plan called for the removal of the nineteenth-century Case Main building, which was finally taken down in the early 1970s. In an attempt to make the most of the limited narrow site, the plan proposed a series of buildings of uniform height around a quadrangle with a horseshoe-shaped group closing the yard at the north end and addressing Euclid Avenue. What was actually built after the war followed the scheme only in the most general way. Ten new buildings developed a quadrangle, but the closure of the north end was only awkwardly accomplished by the Crawford Hall tower. However, one building by Walker and Weeks was built for the Case School, the campus social center, Tomlinson Hall, first planned in 1945 and erected in 1947–48. Tomlinson, probably designed by Dana Clark, seems to have been a conscious essay in reconciling the traditional classicism and the modernistic tendencies in Walker and Weeks's work. At the very least, it pays homage

St. Ann's Catholic Church, Cleveland
Heights, 1949–51.

to their 1926 Medical Library immediately to the east of the campus. The
facade appears classically balanced, though it is actually unsymmetrical,
because the projecting entrance vestibule dominates the front. Another
allegorical sculpture stands above the entrance stairhall window, and the
ranks of windows are divided by shallow pilasters. On the rear facade a
change in grade gives the building three stories, so that the role of the
pilasters in articulating the wall is even more evident. Inside the building,
streamlined aluminum railings once more recall the thirties' ocean-liner
aesthetic. Yet the two-story entrance hall is a restatement of the Allen
Library's stairhall, except that the stair is reversed, with the landing on the
outside wall instead of the inside wall. In the main lounge, there are references to Severance Hall across the street: four square pillars become

St. Ann's Catholic Church, Cleveland Heights, interior. David Thum photo, ca. 1975.

indirect-lighting torcheres with flaring, reeded outlines like those on the Severance auditorium proscenium. The effect of the interior is an appropriately gracious yet relaxed atmosphere, and the ensemble of exterior and interior accomplishes a subtle recapitulation of the classic and modernistic phases of the architects' career.

In 1947, the same year that Tomlinson was built and the Bond store opened, construction began on a building that completed a twenty-year story of delay and frustration and at the same time provides a fitting coda to the classical work of Walker and Weeks. In 1925 Father John M. Powers, of St. Ann's Parish in Cleveland Heights, walked into the First National Bank in Cleveland, which had been built from plans by J. Milton Dyer's office in 1904–6 and was shortly to be torn down as a result of the giant Union Trust merger. Father Powers admired the magnificent Ionic columns, chandeliers, bronze railings, and other architectural elements and purchased them for possible use in a new church. He then commissioned Walker and Weeks to design St. Ann's Church around these elements. The first plan, drawn in 1927, by Dana Clark, displayed a facade based on Provençal Romanesque models. The next year a second version was drawn that changed the plan into a completely Roman basilica like the fifth-century Santa Maria Maggiore in Rome.

The records of the Catholic Diocese indicate that Powers, without diocesan permission, went so far as to have a plaster model made of the proposed church. When Bishop Schrembs received Powers's request to go ahead in 1929, his Council of Administrators determined that the construction would cost more than $700,000. Moreover, the bishop solicited a criticism of the plan from Comes and McMullen of Pittsburgh, who, incidentally, had designed Cleveland's St. Agnes Church in the Provençal Romanesque style. The architects advised that Powers's plan without its altars and other church furniture, did not have "the character of a church."[55] In other words, Schrembs's decision not to approve the building, based primarily on the cost, was bolstered as well by the opinion that the plan looked too much like a secular building, even though the parts salvaged from the bank were not mentioned.

When Bishop Schrembs died in 1945 and was succeeded by Bishop Hoban, Father Powers finally gained permission to begin his classical basilica. The history of its planning explains why the church erected in 1947–52 has always struck observers as dated. The completed building is essentially from the design of 1928. The exterior has a great Ionic portico with a sculptured pediment, a basilican profile, and a tall campanile. The bell tower is somewhat blunter in profile than the one in the original drawings, which was nearly identical with the tower executed on the First Church of Christ, Scientist, in 1929. On the interior the elements from the bank are clearly identifiable, and the ensemble, with its colonnaded aisles, coffered ceiling, and semi-circular apse, creates a very convincing Roman church.

Meanwhile, Walker's interest in residential work for his neighbors and friends continued until the end of his life. Among many others he worked in the early depression years on alterations for the Kirtland estate of Charles H. Strong, president of William Taylor Son & Company, and the drawings for Strong's house are among the few that are actually signed "F.R.W." The last job for which drawings exist by Walker himself was a design for a living-room fireplace mantel and bookcases for William Davidson's Chagrin Falls home. Dated August 10, 1948, they bear the notation "for Bill Davidson. 'Master Craftsman' (not a butcher)."

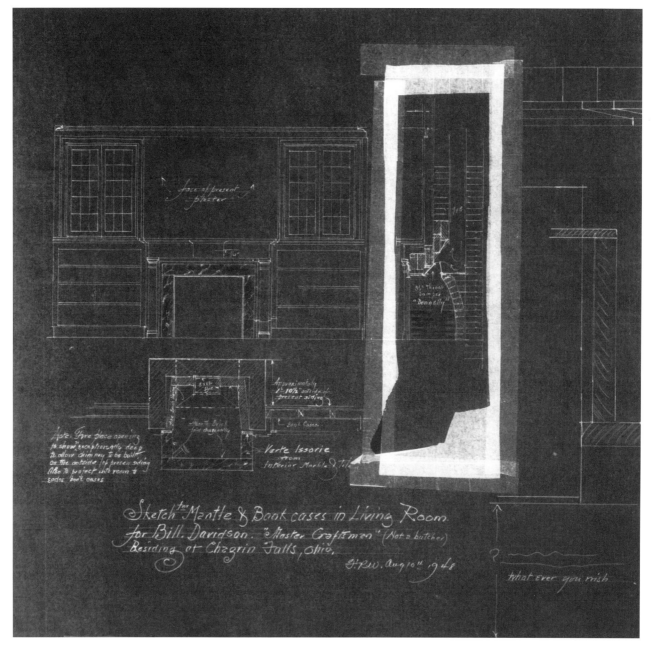

Alterations to the Bill Davidson Residence,
Chagrin Falls, 1948.

Frank Ray Walker died on July 9, 1949, at the age of seventy-one. His obituary appeared on the front page of the *Cleveland Plain Dealer*, which was remarkable for an architect. His twenty-nine honorary pallbearers included several colleagues from the office; business associates Samuel H. Halle and Albert M. Higley; Chagrin Valley friends Crispin Oglebay, George Brown, Bill Davidson, and Courtney Burton; and architects Abram Garfield, Philip Small, Joseph L. Weinberg, and Alex C. Robinson III.

After Walker's death, Howard F. Horn and Frank E. Rhinehart, both of whom had been with Walker since 1919, operated the successor firm that continued in operation for more than twenty years. They remained in the office at 1240 Huron Road where Walker and Weeks moved in December 1941 because the upper floors of the 2341 Carnegie Building were leased to a long-term tenant, Pennsylvania Greyhound. For business purposes they retained the name of Walker and Weeks until 1953, when the partnership became Horn and Rhinehart. They continued in business until 1971, and their work included additions to the Cuyahoga County Hospital buildings in Warrensville, Ohio (originally designed by Milton Dyer), William Taylor Son & Company's suburban store at Southgate shopping center in Maple Heights, Forest City Hospital in Cleveland, and additional new buildings for the Cleveland Boys' School in Hudson, Ohio.

CONCLUSION

THE CAREERS and the buildings of Walker and Weeks speak for themselves. There is almost no writing by either Frank Walker or Harry Weeks on the subject of architecture, aesthetics, style, or any such related matters. There does exist a paper by Walker, apparently written around 1929, that is a fairly specialized essay on the characteristics of various building stones, especially marble, and on the architect's choice and use of them. Yet in this paper the reader can discern certain underlying assumptions that illuminate the entire practice of the period. For example, the essay begins with a passage in which the yearning for classical permanence is made clear.

> When men began to build with permanent materials, it was then, and only then, that he began to register history so that those who lived many centuries later could read with any degree of precision, his habits and tastes. Hence the nations who constructed in a permanent manner are now considered the great nations of antiquity while those whose habits dictated other expressions of activity than permanent buildings are now lacking any enduring records *and* in all probability are even *entirely* forgotten.[56]

It is also noteworthy that the discussion of various kinds of imported stone refers to the great buildings of Western civilization with the confident assumption that the reader will recognize them—whether Greek and Egyptian monuments, Roman temples, or Italian churches—as well as the historical place-names of the Mediterranean region. At the very least, Walker assumed a classically educated audience.

Walker's discussion of the selection of materials, and his knowledge of their sources, expresses the architect's care for every detail. In selecting a building stone, the architect has to know not only its source but the quality of the stock, whether the quantity required could be matched, the cost and availability of labor at the quarry, whether the quarrying was seasonal, the shipping facilities, and the time required for delivery. Walker explicitly insisted that this is not the contractor's business but "most decidedly" the architect's.

Thus, the architect's job is a "hands-on" one. Instead of buying material from a catalog or a dealer's demonstration, the architect should go to the stone yard and make his own selection; moreover, he should go early in the day, "an hour or so before the boss sometimes works to your advantage." Walker described in detail the difficulties encountered in selecting the proper stock and quantity for the lobby of the Federal Reserve Bank in Cleveland. They chose the Sienna marble because of its availability, but after delays in decision making, coupled with shipping problems, "three months of incessant traveling were required" to ensure the selection of the proper quality and amount. Walker concluded by recommending that four years could be allowed to select the stone and achieve an even matching for such a job.

We can conclude from this concern for materials, among other things, that the architect of these buildings considered himself a craftsman. Charles Stark remarked, referring to a residence that Stark not only designed but for which he also made the working drawings, wrote the specifications, and supervised the construction, "it was wonderful practicing architecture at that time—we designed everything, even the doors."[57] The ultimate responsibility of the architect to the client was to see that he got the best design, the best results, and the best materials and workmanship for his money.

It is significant that Walker and Weeks's method was based partly on the Renaissance ideal of craftsmanship and the collaboration between artisans and artists and partly on the modern idea of business. On the one hand, the work was divided in such a way that each member of the team had a sense of accomplishment for his task. This is borne out by the fact that so many of Walker and Weeks's partners and employees stayed for years and even for lifetime careers. On the other hand, the organization of the office, the development of team production, the planning of research and marketing, and the relationships with corporate clients represented the faith in the principle of scientific management that began to dominate business thinking in the early twentieth century.

It is difficult to grasp the size of Walker and Weeks's operations, even in comparison with the large firms seventy years later. A fascinating glimpse of the productivity of the "architectural factory" can be gotten by looking at one year's projects. These are all jobs that were in the early or middle phases of conceptual design or working drawings. In addition, they were working on other commissions in various stages, from preliminary talks with clients to final on-site job supervision.

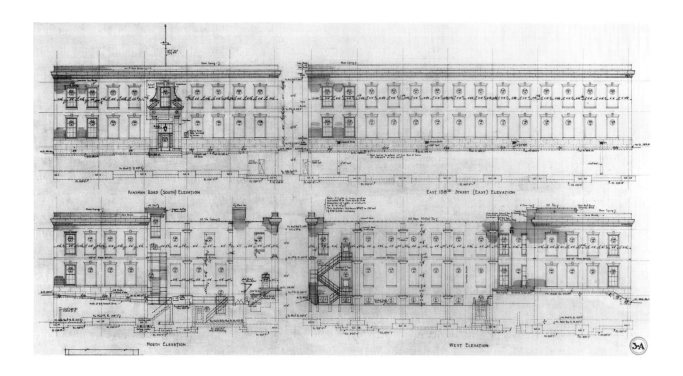

Morningside Office, Ohio Bell Telephone
Company, 1926.

The year is 1926, at the height of Walker and Weeks's career. In January the drawings of Halle's new Prospect Avenue building and bridge were being completed. At the same time a proposal was being prepared for a Presbyterian church in Wooster, Ohio, an interesting case because it is an example of a speculative design, eventually turning out to be one of several, where another architect was finally selected. In February the office was making the drawings for an Ohio Bell Telephone branch exchange in Shaker Heights; its Georgian style was chosen to harmonize with the restrictive guidelines of the planned suburb. The Lee-More Building, a combination store and apartment building also under way in Shaker Heights, was designed in the Tudor revival style, which was unusual for Walker and Weeks but was an acceptable alternative for the Van Sweringen Company. The remodeling of executive offices for the Coca-Cola headquarters in Atlanta was being planned, and in the spring both the Hathaway Brown School and an addition to a department store in Lorain, Ohio, were being designed. Also in progress were the large addition to the Hollenden Hotel, the Greater Wesleyan College campus in Georgia, the Federal Reserve Bank in Cincinnati, work on six branch buildings for the Cleveland Public Library, the beautiful little downtown commercial building for Wolfe's Music Store, and an addition and alterations for a Cadillac dealership in Cleveland.

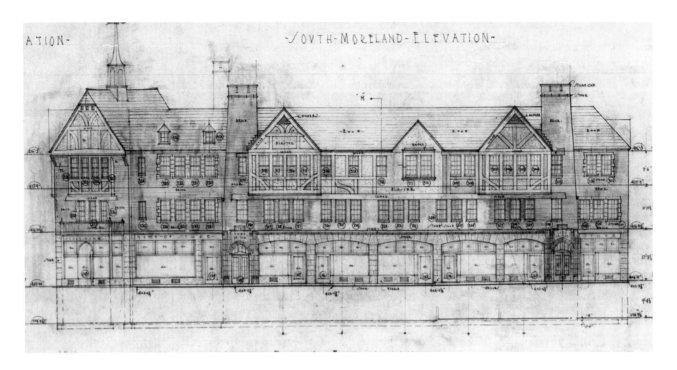

·SOVTH·MORELAND·ELEVATION·

Lee-More Building, Shaker Heights, 1926,
proposed design for Lee Road elevation.

Much of the office's time and energy was occupied by the planning
and details of the Indiana World War Memorial, the enormous undertaking that involved many of the people in the office for twenty years. Several small Ohio jobs occupied the office during the summer, including a
proposed department store in Barberton, a small bank in Bellefontaine,
and another bank in Hillsboro. The autumn brought the commission for
a six-story office building back in Pittsfield, Massachusetts, Walker's hometown. And finally, plans were under way for the Carnegie Building that
became Walker and Weeks's own headquarters.

It would also be difficult to overestimate the importance of Walker and
Weeks's business contacts. This steady stream of commissions came from
clients who made up a veritable *Who's Who* of the wealthy and influential of Cleveland, Ohio, and the Midwest. The local names are familiar
to Clevelanders: the Hannas, Oglebays, and Grassellis in mining, shipping, and chemicals; Squire and Ginn in law; Creech, Treadway, and
Sherwin in banking; the Halles, Strongs, and Binghams in retail and
wholesale trade; the Whites, Warner, and Swasey in manufacturing; and
others equally well known in accounting, publishing, insurance, real estate, and building construction. The fact that dozens of business executives also commissioned their residences from Walker and Weeks is another index of the architects' close ties with the business community.
Walker himself belonged to the major businessmen's and social clubs—
the Union Club, the Hermit Club, the Athletic Club, and the Chagrin

Valley Hunt Club, among others—and certainly much of the business was conducted informally in these centers of power.

The teams that carried out these commissions comprised an exceptional pool of talent, and the caliber of the architects that Walker and Weeks attracted is shown by the number of remarkable alumni that the office produced. Among those who continued in the classical tradition was Munroe W. Copper Jr., who joined the firm when he arrived in Cleveland in 1921 but stayed only briefly. He later set up a partnership with Donald O. Dunn, also from Walker and Weeks. Copper became known for the hundreds of residences that he designed, and especially for his adaptation of Pennsylvania colonial domestic architecture, as well as some fifty-nine churches. Like Walker, he was a resident of Gates Mills and was influential in its planning and development.

Harold B. Burdick worked briefly for Walker and Weeks around 1920, but he is best known for the international-style design of his own residence in Cleveland Heights in 1938. Byron Dalton, who was with Walker and Weeks since 1912 and worked as their principal bank contact and salesman, set up his own office in 1941. Joined by his three sons and nephew, he founded the firm of Dalton-Dalton Associates in 1947. The successor firm is now URS Consultants.

In spite of the economic climate in 1931, Charles H. Stark was hired by Walker and Weeks to design a residence for an Akron banker. When many men were finally laid off because of the depression, Stark began his own practice in partnership with Wilbur H. Adams, Walker and Weeks's chief delineator. Stark left Cleveland for Toledo in 1936, and Adams continued in practice as an industrial designer.

George Voinovich was a draftsman for Walker and Weeks in the mid-1930s, leaving in 1938 to set up an office with John Miller, another of the office draftsmen. Voinovich took with him a church commission he had been working on; St. Lawrence Catholic Church was dedicated in 1940. Armen H. Tashjian, Walker and Weeks's chief engineer for many years, became consulting engineer for the Union Metal Manufacturing Company in Canton in 1938. C. Merrill Barber joined Walker and Weeks as structural engineer in 1930, then set up his own office in 1934, but remained their consulting engineer until he formed his own partnership in 1942, which became Barber and Hoffman in 1965.

The most illustrious alumnus was probably J. Byers Hays, who joined Walker and Weeks in 1920 after coming to Cleveland from the office of Raymond Hood in New York. In interviews shortly before his death in 1968, Hays discussed his responsibility for the design of the Federal Reserve Bank in Cleveland, the Cleveland Municipal Stadium, and the winning competition design for the Indiana World War Memorial. In

1930 Hays set up his own office and was later joined by Byron Hunsicker, a construction superintendent with Walker and Weeks, and Russell Simpson to form Hays, Simpson & Hunsicker. Hays's work took a much more modern direction with innovative structures for the Great Lakes Exposition, the master plan for the Cleveland Zoo, and the 1958 addition to the Cleveland Museum of Art.

Frank Walker, Harry Weeks, and their partners lived up to the conclusion that had already been made by 1914, a judgment that was in no way premature: "Mr. Walker and Mr. Weeks have taught the most difficult lesson of all . . . a building must be a distinctly artistic creation, but must also be a commercial and business success and serve well the purposes for which it is designed."[58] While they eloquently and infallibly expressed the temper of their own times, Walker and Weeks also maintained the faith that they were firmly on the road to a "new architecture." Their sense of style was integral with the program and the meaning of their buildings, never a gratuitous display or a mere attempt to keep up with avant-garde fashion. Their designs have the power to delight the viewer today as much as they did fifty, sixty, seventy years ago. This was the testament of the fortuitous partnership that brought two young men from Massachusetts—an unassuming, competent manager, Harry E. Weeks, and a brilliant, outgoing architect, Frank R. Walker—to transform a great Midwestern city.

APPENDIX: CATALOG OF COMMISSIONS

T HE FOLLOWING is a catalog of commissions from the office of Walker and Weeks between the founding of the firm in 1911 and Walker's death in 1949. It is arranged in chronological order by the earliest date that may be assigned for the design of a project, rather than the construction date. In this way it will be easy for the reader to follow any evolution in the firm's work that may be apparent. Only in some instances is it possible to attribute design responsibility, but it must be kept in mind that there were several architectural designers in the firm. The catalog includes buildings that are known to have been executed, unbuilt projects, and projects whose outcome is unknown. Wherever possible, the present status of the building is given. "Extant," "demolished," and "unbuilt" are clear; "not extant" means that there is insufficient evidence to indicate whether the project was executed or not. If not otherwise indicated, the location of the project was Cleveland, Ohio. In addition to those cataloged, there were numerous other jobs, such as the minor remodeling of existing buildings, consultations on proposals that never came to fruition, and jobs for which there is insufficient record to warrant a descriptive entry.

This catalog is largely based on the collection of Walker and Weeks's records in the library of The Western Reserve Historical Society. The collection includes thousands of preliminary sketches, working drawings in ink on linen, blueprints, contractors' drawings, and photographs, plus correspondence, job records, articles by members of the firm, critical reviews, and other manuscript material. At the time the collection was acquired by the library, it had been abandoned and stored under adverse conditions for several years. Therefore, the information available is not assumed to be complete; the projects cited may be no more than a portion of the actual output of the firm.

George N. Sherwin Residence 11898 Carlton Road. Designed 1911–12. Shingled residence with center hall plan. One of several houses for the Carlton Park development. Built for a vice president of the Union Trust Company. Demolished.

James H. Foster Residence 2200 Devonshire Drive at Chestnut Hills, Cleveland Heights. Designed 1911–12, alterations 1917. Large stucco residence with central hall plan, with unusual placement of den in front of the hall. Has double-gable facade common in Walker & Weeks's residences, probably influenced by C. F. A. Voysey. Extant.

American Baptist Mission Swatow, China (coastal city north of Hong Kong). Designed 1912. Features an arched stone gateway to the mission compound. Alternate sketches show a gabled tile roof. Inscribed tablet "Founded by William Ashmore 1860." Ashmore was an Ohio Baptist missionary. Status unknown.

Louis J. Grossman Residence 10519 Lake Shore Boulevard at Doan Avenue, Bratenahl. Designed 1912. Alterations and additions to an existing house, including porch, deck, kitchen, and basement utiliites. Demolished.

Community Mausoleum Designed 1909 by J. Milton Dyer and revised in 1912 by Walker & Weeks. Classical mausoleum in the Doric order with a cross-shaped plan. Designed for the Cleveland Mausoleum Company, president Edwin Blandin of Blandin, Rice & Ginn.

Mausoleum from this design erected in Brooklyn Heights Cemetery, Broadview Road, Cleveland. Demolished.

Mausoleum from this design erected in Lakewood Park Cemetery, 22025 Detroit Road, Rocky River, Ohio. Granite construction. Extant.

Cuyahoga Builders Supply Warehouses Dubroy (Quebec) Avenue, Cleveland; Hird Avenue, Lakewood; Collinwood. Designed 1912. Dubroy Avenue warehouse included a stable with fourteen stalls and a central air shaft. Not extant.

National Car Wheel Company Foundry 2112 West 106th Street. Designed 1909 by J. B. Hayes (*not* J. Byers Hays). Drawings show framing details of building and plans of foundry, cupola house, pit house, and cleaning house. Annealing pits designed 1912 by Walker & Weeks. Demolished.

George Edmondson Store Building Designed 1912. Commercial facade of brick piers and large display windows for attachment to an existing house at 2362 Euclid Avenue. Planned for a leading Cleveland photographer (1866–1948). Unbuilt.

Mrs. James M. Jones Residence 11896 Carlton Road. Designed 1912. Frame colonial center hall residence with a three-bay facade and a four-column portico. Palladian rear elevation overlooked Cedar Glen. Garage added 1922 for Miss Myrta L. Jones. Demolished.

F. W. Judd Residence 2465 Marlboro Road at Fairfax Road, Cleveland Heights. Magnificent brick residence with a double-gable facade, massive hip roof, and an arcaded terrace. Complete final drawings were executed for two versions, the first in April 1912, the second in August 1912. Extant.

B. R. Baker Store, 1912–13.

The Shaker Heights Improvement Company Plan for "Marlboro Park" between Fairmount and Fairfax, dated May 1912, included residences by architects Meade and Hamilton, Page and Corbusier, F. W. Striebinger, and Walker & Weeks.

National City Bank 51–53 South Main Street, Akron, Ohio. Designed 1912. Bank with a central banking room and a facade of two Corinthian columns in antis, two pilasters, and a parapet balustrade, analogous to J. Milton Dyer's First National Bank, Cleveland (1906). Demolished.

Sandusky County Courthouse Fremont, Ohio. Designed 1912. Proposed design for a monumental two-story neoclassic courthouse with Corinthian portico, low Roman dome, grand entrance staircase and recumbent lions. For the block bounded by Park, Croghan, Court, and Clover Streets. Preliminary sketch plans and two color renderings on linen in the beaux-arts style of illustration were executed. Unbuilt.

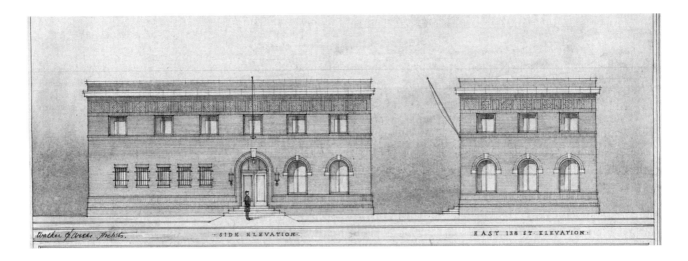

·SIDE ELEVATION·   ·EAST 138 ST ELEVATION·

Fourteenth Precinct Station, Cleveland Police Department, 1912–13.

Renkert Building North Market and East Fourth Streets, Canton, Ohio. Designed 1912–13. Ten-story commercial building with four bays on Market and sixteen on Fourth Street. Emphasis on strong vertical brick piers, recessed spandrels, and an arcaded corbeled cornice. Steel framing by Riverside Bridge Company, Martins Ferry, Ohio. Extant.

B. R. Baker Store 1001 Euclid Avenue. Retail store building designed 1912–13 by altering the experimental John Hartness Brown Building (1901). Additional alterations made 1938. Extant. Altered.

Cleveland Police Department 14th Precinct Building East 138th Street and Idarose. Designed 1912–13. Two-story building with muster room, officers' rooms, jail, and second-story locker room and dining room. A patterned brick exterior with round-arched openings. Demolished.

Korach Company Factory Superior Avenue at East 24th Street. Designed 1912–13. Two-story garment factory with stock room, cutting room, sewing room. Facade with brick piers; enclosed water tower; concrete mushroom column construction. Extant. Altered.

C. A. Maher Residence 1949 East 93rd Street. Designed 1912. Alterations to an existing house. Remodeled entrance hall and sleeping porch. Garage added 1914. Demolished.

Kinney and Levan Building 1375 Euclid Avenue. Designed 1912–13. Six-story, classical retail store building, one of the first at Playhouse Square. Elegant art nouveau interior details. (Later Stouffer Building; One Playhouse Square) Extant.

Leader-News *Building Offices* Superior Avenue at East 6th Street. Building designed 1911–12 by Charles A. Platt. M. A. Hanna offices designed by Walker & Weeks 1914, and lobby details 1917. Additional alterations for M. A. Hanna Company 1927. Building extant.

National City Bank Leader-News *Building.* Designed 1913. Large banking room with a Superior Avenue entrance and connected to the building arcade. Coffered ceilings with skylights. Building extant. Altered.

Loomis Building 1021–1031 Euclid Avenue. Designed March 1913. Alterations for the easternmost retail store (Stearns) in the experimental John Hartness Brown Building (see B. R. Baker Store). Classical terra-cotta facade detail. Additional alterations 1917. Also major structural, mechanical, and interior design remodeling for Stearns, 1943. Extant. Altered.

Benedict Crowell Residence 10710 Magnolia Drive. Designed July 1913–January 1914. Large stucco mansion in the Renaissance revival style with a long narrow floor plan and a side porte-cochere entrance. Six bedrooms and several servants' rooms. One of several residences that included a patented steam heating system. Built for assistant secretary of war under Newton D. Baker, president of Crowell-Lundoff Construction, and president of Central National Bank. Demolished (Veterans Administration Hospital site).

Frank E. Abbott Residence Carlton Road. Designed December 1913. Large shingled house with five roof dormers and a bow-shaped columned portico. Center hall interior plan with a reverse stair at the entrance. Demolished.

Stillman Building 1101 Euclid Avenue. Designed November–December 1913. Six-story retail (Siegel's) and office building with extraordinary terra-cotta detail, bronze and polychrome terra-cotta entrance. Benedict Crowell was vice president of Stillman Company. Terra-cotta by Northwestern Terra Cotta Company. Extant. Facade destroyed.

Frank C. Newcomer Cottage County Line Road, Gates Mills, Ohio. Designed December 1913. One-and-a-half-story rustic cottage of Swiss chalet design, with vertical siding, two-story living room, and massive stone chimney. Newcomer a founder of the Chagrin Valley Hunt Club. Not extant.

Western Reserve National Bank Market and Main Streets, Warren, Ohio. Designed 1913. Seven-story bank building with two two-story columns in antis. Plans are signed: "OK F.R.W." Extant. Altered.

Rainbow Cottage 1605 South Green Road, South Euclid, Ohio. Designed 1913. New buildings for Rainbow Babies and Children's Hospital. Two-story stucco building plus basement, with an axial corridor flanked by wards. Demolished.

H. C. Milligan Residence 1522 Cleveland Avenue NW, Canton, Ohio. Designs 1913. Alterations to an existing house, changing a typical foursquare house to a colonial revival residence. Extant. Altered.

Painter Residence Essex Road, Gates Mills. Designed 1913. U-shaped residence with family wing and servants' wing flanking a court. Altered 1929 for A. W. Russell, with original gambrel roof replaced by a gable with Greek revival detail. Destroyed.

Louis N. Weber Residence 2860 Euclid Heights Boulevard, Cleveland Heights. Designed ca. 1913. Foursquare house with hip roof, two-column entry stoop, glassed-in breakfast room, and exposed fieldstone basement on sloping site. For the president of Weber, Lind & Hall, interior decorators. Demolished (Coventry School site).

Raymond Hitchcock Residence Great Neck, Long Island, New York. Designed 1913. Alterations and additions to an existing house, including a large living room, great bay window, and autograph gallery. For a prominent stage actor, contemporary of Lillian Russell and George M. Cohan. Status unknown.

S. Prentiss Baldwin House Gates Mills, Ohio. Measured drawings of an existing colonial-style house (pre-1903) and a garden plan in 1913; a classical entry porch 1917; barn alterations, 1918; and farmer's cottage, 1924. For the lawyer and early developer of Gates Mills. Extant. Altered.

Mrs. Henry L. Sanford Residence 11930 Carlton Road. Designed 1913–14. Stucco cottage with gabled roof and rustic recessed porch. Center hall interior plan with a bow window in the living room. For a founder of the Women's City Club. Demolished.

Warner & Swasey Exposition Booth Panama-Pacific Exposition, San Francisco, California, 1915. Designed 1914. Small classical pavilion with ornamental astronomical signs, in which the telescope later installed in the Case School Observatory was displayed. Located in the Palace of Machinery. Temporary structure. Dismantled.

Max McMurray Residence 12521 Lake Shore Boulevard, Bratenahl, Ohio. Designed January 1914. Large and imposing stucco Mediterranean villa with an arcaded veranda and a long narrow plan parallel to the lake. Additions 1916. Extant.

Malcolm L. McBride Residence 1583 Mistletoe Drive. Designed February 1914. Additions and alterations to an existing house, consisting of a wing with storeroom, pantry, porch, and two bedrooms. Original house 1909 by Briggs and Nelson. Designed for president of Root & McBride Company. Demolished.

English Woolen Mills Company Store 232 Superior Avenue NE. Designed March 1914. Alterations for a store facade in the Cuyahoga Building (1893), including a leaded glass transom of art nouveau derivation. Demolished.

Union National Bank Building 308 Euclid Avenue. Designed March 1914. Seventeen-story classical bank building with an arcaded banking hall. Additional designs were made in 1918, after the change to Union Commerce National Bank, for a tower based on the Giralda, Seville. Demolished.

Walter W. Dennis Residence Gates Mills. Designed June 1914. Small rectangular stucco residence with a rooftop pergola. Status unknown.

Four-Suite Apartment for Lester Jacobson Hower Avenue, East Cleveland, Ohio. Designed March–July 1914. Apartment building with a center entrance and two half-timbered bracketed gables in the arts and crafts idiom. Alternate scheme in neoclassic style was made. Not extant.

St. Mary's College Garage North East, Pennsylvania. Designed July 1914. Two-story garage building with a workshop on the lower grade level. Status unknown.

Haltnorth Building and Theatre Woodland Avenue at East 55th Street. Designed August 1914. Complex of two buildings, a three-story retail building on East 55th Street and a theater building on Haltnorth Court. Theater with a capacity of 1,280, a stage thirty feet deep, and a lobby, auditorium, and proscenium ornamented with rich classical detail. On the site of Haltnorth's Gardens. Demolished.

Andrew Squire Farm Barn Valleevue Farm, 37125 Fairmount Road, Hunting Valley, Ohio. Designed September 1914. Large U-shaped barn with cattle stalls, hay loft, tool and wagon rooms. Built for founder of Squire, Sanders & Dempsey. Extant.

Alwyn C. Ernst Residence 108 Windermere Terrace, East Cleveland. Designed September 1914. Alterations to an existing house for the founder of Ernst & Ernst accounting firm. Demolished.

Oliver W. Renkert Residence 1375 North Market Street, Canton, Ohio. Designed September 1914. Brick residence with arcaded porch and unusually large dormers. For general manager of Metropolitan Paving Brick. Extant (See Renkert Building, 1912).

St. Vincent Charity Hospital Central Avenue at East 22nd Street. Designed September 1914. Meyer J. Sturm, consulting architect, Chicago. Five-story brick and terra-cotta hospital wing whose fifth story is ornamented with a classical colonnade. Interior plan with axial double-loaded corridors, basement dispensary, emergency room, private rooms and wards, consulting and operating rooms, and modern mechanical systems. Extant.

H. D. Horwitz Residence Designed October 1914. Proposal for a large brick hip-roofed house with an arcaded porch, related to the Judd residence (1912). Unusual floor plan with the main living rooms to one side of a stair hall. Designed for the triangular lot on Norfolk Road at Overlook, Cleveland Heights. A second version in 1917 was more conservative in plan. Unbuilt.

George C. Steinemann Residence 1133 Wayne Street, Sandusky, Ohio. Designed November 1914. Various schemes were made for a residence in Georgian or English cottage styles, although the plans for the executed residence do not exist. Extant.

W. Bingham Company Warehouse 1278 West 9th Street. Designed December 1914. Block-long, eight-story, L-shaped steel, concrete, and brick-faceted wholesale warehouse with pier-and-spandrel facades and a simple concave cornice. Steep grade level difference between West 9th and West 10th Streets. Extant.

Henry L. Thompson Residence Dixie Highway, Perrysburg, Ohio. Farmer's cottage for a large estate designed 1914, and the residence 1915. Additional alterations were planned in 1918–19, including a garden pergola. For president of Bostwick-Braun Company. Extant.

William W. Knight Residence Belmont Farms, Perrysburg, Ohio. Farm buildings for an estate planned in 1914 and the residence in 1916. For vice president of Bostwick-Braun Company. Extant.

Cleveland Heights High School Euclid Heights Boulevard. Designed 1914–15. Three-story school building with sets of rooms on a longitudinal corridor, a center auditorium, and a gymnasium on a lower level. Plans for an Ashtabula High School, E. E. Joralemon, architect, were used as reference. Later became Boulevard School. Demolished.

Thomas P. Howell Residence 12304 Coit Road, Bratenahl, Ohio. Designed January 1915. Addition of a Doric four-column porch to an existing house. For the manager of General Chemicals Company. Extant.

Garfield Savings Bank Branches St. Clair Avenue at East 79th Street and East 105th Street. Designed January and April 1915. East 79th Street building is a brick two-story trapezium with Tuscan pilasters on the elevations, a narrow entrance end facing St. Clair, and space on two floors for retail tenants. President Harris Creech became president of Cleveland Trust Company, which acquired the Garfield Bank in 1922. Extant.

F. J. Smith Residence 1615 Sheridan Road, South Euclid, Ohio. Designed February 1915. Unconventional rectangular neo-Greek revival house designed by J. P. Neppel in Walker & Weeks office. Extant.

Frank H. Townsend Bungalow Pensacola, Florida. Designed February 1915. Simple gabled one-story house with an open porch and living rooms, bedrooms, and servants' quarters on one floor. Status unknown.

Mrs. John Nash Residence 2611 Guilford Road, Cleveland Heights. Designed March 1915. Brick Georgian house with a hip roof. Unusual relieving arches over the front windows were not built as shown in plans. John Nash was an officer of the Cleveland Provision Company. Extant. Altered.

Walter S. Bowler Residence 2911 South Park, Shaker Heights, Ohio. Designed May 1915. Large L-shaped shingled house with a long living-room facade facing the street and a steep hip roof with dormers sloping down to extend over the side porch. Kitchen, pantry, and servants' rooms in the rear ell. Built for vice president of Lake Shore Banking and Trust Company. Extant. Altered.

William H. Hunt Cottage Hemlock Road, South Park Station, Independence, Ohio. Alterations June 1915 to an existing arts-and-crafts-style bungalow by Albert Skeel. For president of Cleveland Life Insurance Company. Extant.

Hospital Norwalk, Ohio. Designed July 1915. Proposed alterations to the Poyer House, a nineteenth-century residence at 61 Norwood Avenue, for medical consulting, surgery, and patient care. Hospital unbuilt. House extant.

Amusement Palace Designed September 1915. Proposal for a four-story theater, physical club, bowling alley, and ballroom building 180 feet long between Erie Court and Bolivar Road, Cleveland. Unbuilt.

Mrs. Nelson B. Sherwin Residence 320 Corning Drive, Bratenahl, Ohio. Designed October 1915. Shingled colonial revival house with a five-bay facade, a simple Greek-style entry porch, and an attached garage. Interior center hall plan with kitchen and servants' quarters linked to garage. Extant.

Francis E. Drury Estate Drury Lane, Willoughby Township, Lake County, Ohio. Designed September 1915. Several proposed buildings for a country estate, including a two-story garage building on a sloping site. Club house and little theater planned April 1916. Tea House, September 1918, was a picturesque octagonal random-ashlar and half-timbered outbuilding. Unbuilt. Also planned a garage for Drury's Cleveland house at 8615 Euclid Avenue, a 1912 residence by Meade and Hamilton.

E. G. Buckwell Residence 2005 Chestnut Hills Drive, Cleveland Heights. Designed November 1915. Brick hip-roofed Georgian mansion with three windows on the street elevation with semicircular terra-cotta lunettes. The main entrance front has a Palladian window, and the garden front has three sets of three-part French windows. Extant.

W. H. Prescott Residence 3097 Fairmount Boulevard, Cleveland Heights. Designed December 1915. Symmetrical brick colonial house with end gables and double chimneys, five bays of arched windows, and three roof dormers. Extant.

C. E. Morganthaler Residence 1896 East 79th Street. Designed ca. 1915. Alterations and additions to an existing house. Draftsman: F.R.W. Extant. Also prepared plans for Morganthaler residence in Geneva, Illinois, 1916.

Guardian Building 623 Euclid Avenue. The New England Building (1895, Shepley, Rutan & Coolidge, Boston; one of the finest early tall office buildings in Cleveland) remodeled 1915 for Guardian Savings & Trust. Facade of colossal Corinthian columns replaced the arched entrance. A majestic banking room on the basilican plan with coffered ceiling and Corinthian columns, ornamented in marble, bronze, and gold. A seventeen-story addition extended the building to Vincent Avenue. Steel grillage, columns, and girders by Ambridge Steel Company. Extant.

Short Creek Coal Company Store Cadiz, Ohio, vicinity. Date unknown, probably ca. 1915. Rectangular one-and-a-half-story store building with gambrel roof and dormers, a main general store room, a smaller store room, a meat store, and a workroom. Cleveland office in the *Leader-News* Building. Status unknown.

Lorain County Savings and Trust Middle Avenue, Elyria, Ohio. Designed March 1916. Eleven-story brick-faced bank and office building with corbelled cornice and a first-story facade of fourstone Tuscan columns. Also planned an addition when changed to First National Bank, 1920. Extant.

Charles N. Hickok Residence 12505 Coit Road, Bratenahl. Designed April 1916. Center hall brick colonial house with a lengthwise facade and glassed-in sun porch. Built for an executive of M. A. Hanna Company. Extant.

Young Women's Christian Association 1710 Prospect Avenue. Designed May 1916. Alterations to the existing 1908 building by Levi T. Scofield. Addition of swimming pool, locker rooms and recreation room to the south and west and connected to an existing residence. Extant. Several schemes were made for a separate classical building south of the alley.

Arthur D. Brooks Residence 11936 Carlton Road. Designed June 1916. Unsymmetrical shingled colonial design with steep roof, two-and-a-half stories, and a central hall plan. Brooks was the secretary of Brooks Company stationers. Demolished.

Grasselli Chemical Company Office North 13th Street, Terre Haute, Indiana. Designed August 1916. A one-story hip-roof office building. One of many branch offices of the important Cleveland chemical company. Not extant.

Cleveland Public Auditorium St. Clair Avenue and East 6th Street. Designed October 1916. Frederic H. Betz and J. Harold MacDowell, city architects, with Frank Walker, consulting architect. Large arena and exhibition hall in Renaissance style. Constructed 1920–22. South wing (Music Hall) 1927–28 by Herman Kregelius, city architect. Extant.

Frank Billings Residence 11136 Magnolia Drive. Designed November 1916. Large yellow brick, center hall mansion with an arcaded loggia, stone Tuscan columns, and extensive servants' quarters. For the president of Tod-Stambaugh Company, the Mahoning Valley coal and iron-ore company. Extant.

Arthur D. Brooks Residence 11936 Carlton Place. Designed November 1916. For the secretary of Brooks Company, stationers. Demolished.

Proposed Building for H. T. Loomis & Company. Designed December 1916. Proposed ten-story doctors' and dentists' building with a facade of vertical gothic lines for the northwest corner of Euclid Avenue and East 18th Street. Various schemes were made for retail shops on the first story and offices on the upper floors. Unbuilt.

Frank Billings residence, 1916.

F. R. Hazard Bungalow Lake Cazenovia, near Syracuse, New York. Designed 1916. One-and-a-half-story rustic shingled hip-roof cottage, with a large living room, six bedrooms, and two sleeping porches on one level. Status unknown.

Park Drive Apartments Park Drive (Martin Luther King Jr. Boulevard) and East 107th Street. Designed 1916. Numerous sketches and plans were made for a proposed chateau-style luxury apartment building overlooking the Fine Arts lagoon (Epworth-Euclid Methodist Church site). Unbuilt.

Cleveland Public Library 325 Superior Avenue NE. Competition plan 1916. Walker & Weeks won the competition over two local and five national architects for a building complementing the Federal Courthouse at the south end of the Group Plan Mall. Five-story marble facades with an arcaded ground story and colossal colonnades in the Renaissance style. Vaulted lobby and main reading room on a monumental scale. Fifteen reading rooms with open stacks; forty-seven miles of shelving. Design attributed to Claude W. Stedman. Working designs August 1919; revisions through 1923. Extant.

Ames Company Store Building 240 Euclid Avenue. Six-story retail building altered 1916–17 with a storefront of classical and art nouveau detail. Original design 1914 by Starrett and Van Vleck, New York. Extant. Altered.

Mortimer C. Rosenfeld Residence 1706 Magnolia Drive. Designed February 1917. Additions to an existing house (possibly by Walker & Weeks) in the arts and crafts idiom. New dining room, kitchen, pantry, and nursery wing. Built for the treasurer of Grabler Manufacturing. Demolished.

American Express Company Garage Lakeside Avenue at East 17th Street. Designed March 1917. Distinguished design consisting of a large steel-post and beam structure with brick exterior walls, and containing truck garage, repair shop, and offices. Extant.

Mrs. Dean (Virginia) Holden Residence 11239 Lake Shore Boulevard, Bratenahl, Ohio. Designed April 1917. Additions and alterations to an existing house, including utility wing with laundry, kitchen, flower room, and servants' room. Demolished.

Central Savings and Trust Company Building 102–106 South Main Street, Akron, Ohio. Designed April 1917. Extensive alterations to the existing six-story gothic-style Hamilton Building, especially for the main banking floor. Demolished. (Central Savings and Trust site, 1929.)

Charles L. Murfey Residence 16300 South Park Boulevard, Shaker Heights, Ohio. Designed May 1917. Symmetrical brick Georgian house based on Virginia tidewater examples, with a ten-bay facade, hip roof, dormers, and center hall plan. Fully developed garden facade. Built for a vice president of Guardian Savings and Trust. Extant.

Charles F. Lang Residence 1019 Homewood Drive, Lakewood, Ohio. Designed July 1917. Two-and-a-half-story shingled, modified colonial-style house with a primary Georgian facade facing the lake and an elaborate entrance with carved wooden pediment, Tuscan columns, and latticed entry porch. Built for president of Clifton Engineering. Extant.

C. A. Maher Estate Hanover Road, Gates Mills, Ohio. Designed 1917. Large farm barn with U-wings, gambrel roof, and cupola. Not extant. Also planned a two-story rustic lodge on a steep ravine, 1919. Contractor: George W. Brown. (See also Maher residence, 1912.)

Van Sweringen Company Houses Coventry Road at Haddam, Shaker Heights, Ohio. Designed August 1917. Two proposed model homes for Lots 36 and 42 in the Shaker Heights development, both five-bay brick colonial center hall homes. Neither one was built as designed.

Windsor T. White Farm Cottages Halfred Farm, Chagrin River Road at Shaker Boulevard, Hunting Valley, Ohio. Designed September 1917. Large farm complex including a chauffeur and gardener's cottage and a guest cottage with veranda, 1919. Built for the president of White Motor Company. Extant.

Kent National Bank Main and Water Streets, Kent, Ohio. Designed September 1917. Remodeling of the facade and interior of an existing building. Not extant.

Rubber City Savings Bank 1115 South Main Street, Akron, Ohio. Designed November 1917. Two-story bank with a facade of three bays with pilasters. Various alternate schemes were made. President Harvey S. Firestone. Later Firestone Park Savings and Trust. Demolished.

Max Hellman Residence Designed November 1917. Proposed center hall colonial house with elaborate fanlight entrance. Planned for the president of the Lindner Company. The design was built neither at the lot indicated on the plan, 2724 Berkshire Road, nor Hellman's actual address, 2828 Edgehill Road, Cleveland Heights, Ohio.

Garden Apartments for Francis E. Drury Euclid Avenue at East 86th Street. Designed December 1917. Several elaborate schemes were drawn for a six-story apartment building in the Elizabethan style, with common rooms and two large luxury apartments per floor, one of which was intended for the Drurys. Later scheme (1921) shows a lavish apartment group on the entire block between Euclid and Carnegie at East 86th Street (not yet platted). Unbuilt. (Cleveland Play House site.)

First National Bank Superior Avenue opposite East 3rd Street. Designed 1917. Numerous conceptual sketches and plans for remodeling J. Milton Dyer's 1906 bank at 241 Euclid Avenue and extending it through to Superior, with a visionary scheme for a campanile tower on the axis of the Mall. Artist: T. J. Bryson. Unbuilt.

Lorain Banking Company Broadway and Sixth Street, Lorain, Ohio. Designed 1917. Alterations to an existing 1895 Romanesque-style building, consisting of a new classical facade with Doric columns. Extant.

First National Bank Broad Street, Elyria, Ohio. 1917. Designed 1917. Small bank with neoclassic facade and two columns. Also remodeled 1929 (Savings Deposit and Trust Company). Extant.

Walter C. White Estate Circle W Farm, County Line Road, Chester Township, Geauga County, Ohio. Designed 1917. Great country estate, including the main colonial revival house, stable, dairy barn, cottages, and other buildings, continuously modified through 1929. For member of the White Motor Corporation family. Extant (Hawken School).

Robert H. Bishop Jr. Residence County Line Road, Hunting Valley, Ohio. Designed 1917. Proposed schemes for a large classical revival house with porticos. Unbuilt. For the director of University Hospitals, Cleveland. (The existing house was designed 1927 by Coolidge, Shepley, Bullinch & Abbott, Boston.)

Goodyear Tire and Rubber Company Building East Market Street at Goodyear Boulevard, Akron. Designed 1917. Block-long brick six-story employee recreation building for the Goodyear Company, containing gymnasium, theater, cafeteria, bowling alleys, classrooms, offices, and other facilities. Art deco detail and Guastavino tile vaulting. Extant (Goodyear Hall).

Central Savings and Trust 523 West Tuscarawas Street (old 121–123 East), Barberton, Ohio. Designed 1917–18. Two-story bank with two Corinthian columns and containing a long narrow banking room. A six-story version was also drawn. Designer: Dana Clark. Extant. Altered.

Automatic Sprinkler Company Office Building Jones and Brittain Streets, Youngstown, Ohio. Designed January 1918. Two-story brick building containing engineers' rooms, drafting rooms, blueprint rooms, and clerks' offices. Demolished.

George Sheppard Residence Old Mill Road, Gates Mills. Designed April 1918. Alterations and porch addition to the Greek revival Washington Gates house (1854) adjacent to St. Christopher's Church. Extant.

A. A. Augustus Farm Buildings Shaker Boulevard (old South Woodland) at Chagrin River Road, Hunting Valley, Ohio. Designed May 1918. Large picturesque barn with five turrets, a farmer's cottage, and stone walls. Later the Ingalls Estate. Extant.

Alliance Houses Alliance, Ohio. Designed August 1918. Eighty-nine five-, six-, and seven-room square brick houses were built of 181 planned. Workers' housing built by the Bureau of Industrial Housing and Transportation of the U.S. Department of Labor during World War I. Extant.

Lyman H. Treadway Garage 8917 Euclid Avenue. Designed 1918. Large brick garage to complement the existing house by J. Milton Dyer, with steep hip roof, six-car garage, workroom, storeroom, chauffeur's room, tool room, potting room, and greenhouse. Extant (The Health Museum of Cleveland).

First National Bank of Fremont Croghan Street, Fremont, Ohio. Designed 1918. Various schemes were made for the remodeling or complete rebuilding of an existing Victorian Italianate building. Walker & Weeks referred to the original nineteenth-century plans by J. C. Johnson. Demolished.

First National Bank of Bellevue Bellevue, Ohio. Designed 1918–19. Remodeling and addition of a new facade to an existing nineteenth-century building in the Romanesque style. Extant.

Lakewood Engineering Company Office Building Berea Road, Lakewood, Ohio. Designed 1918–19. Designs made for one-story and two-story brick office buildings, both long and narrow with central corridors flanked by offices, the larger one with a classical Tuscan portico. Not extant.

Fairlawn Heights Golf Club West Market Street at Revere Road (old Beck Road), Akron, Ohio. Designed March 1919. Brick gabled country club with a two-story lounge and open-truss ceiling. Landscape architect Warren H. Manning. Destroyed 1929.

Ohio Savings and Trust Building East Market Street at Goodyear Boulevard, Akron, Ohio. Designed April 1919. Three-story Renaissance-style bank building designed to fit the triangular corner adjacent to the Goodyear recreation building (1917). Later Goodyear Bank. F. A. Seiberling, president. Extant.

Dr. Louis E. Sisler Residence and Garage 675 N. Portage Path, Akron, Ohio. Designed May 1919. Large brick residence for the vice president of Firestone Park Trust and Savings Bank. Extant.

Geneva Savings Bank 21 South Broadway, Geneva, Ohio. Designed May 1919. Classical bank with a five-bay stone facade, two Doric columns, and pilasters. Extant.

William Taylor Son & Company Store 630 Euclid Avenue. Designs May 1919. Alterations to the nine-story 1907 store building by J. Milton Dyer, including storefront elevations for the Euclid Avenue facade and the Taylor Arcade. Had also made window details for the first store expansion in 1914. Demolished.

Dr. William W. Bustard Residence 18829 (old 13679) Fairmount Boulevard, Shaker Heights, Ohio. Designed May 1919. Alterations to an existing nineteenth-century Greek revival farmhouse, with new dormers and porches. For the pastor of the Euclid Avenue Baptist Church. Extant.

Garage for W. J. Knapp 7714 Carnegie Avenue. Designed June 1919. One-story brick utilitarian commercial garage building. Demolished.

Cowell and Hubbard Building 1301 Euclid Avenue. Designed July 1919. Two-story classical building for the jewelry specialty store, with retail store rooms, basement, and mezzanine accounting offices. Extant.

Wright Banking Company Building South West and Monroe Streets, Bellevue, Ohio. Designed August 1919. Two-story bank building on an irregular triangular site with classical pilasters on the elevations, and including three retail store spaces. Extant. Altered.

Citizens National Bank Building Mansfield, Ohio. Designed August 1919. Ten-story stone-faced classical bank and office building with arched windows on the elevation. Extant.

Fen-Far Building East 9th Street and Bolivar. Designed September 1919. Extensive alterations to existing buildings, making a four-story T-shaped structure with a light court. Remarkable polychrome terra-cotta entrance facade. Planned for Erie-Huron Realty Company. Not extant.

Proposed Hotel Building East 107th Street. Designed September 1919. Conceptual designs for a proposed nine-story office and commercial hotel building. Designer: C. W. Stedman. Anticipated Fenway Hall, designed in 1922 by George B. Post & Sons. Unbuilt.

Steubenville Bank and Trust Building Market and Fourth Streets, Steubenville, Ohio. Designed October 1919. Twelve-story stone-faced bank and office building with a monumental arcaded ground story. Peterson & Clarke, Steubenville, associated architects. Extant.

Lake Shore Bank Prospect and Huron Road. Designed October 1919. Alterations to exterior elevations and interior plans of the existing Osborn Building. Building extant.

Roger Williams Press Payne Avenue at East 38th Street. Designed November 1919. Alterations and structural reinforcement of an existing nineteenth-century commercial building for the printing company. Building extant.

Woodland Avenue Savings and Trust Designed November–December 1919.
     Woodland and East 55th Street: Alterations to an existing building (ca. 1885). Demolished.
     Kinsman and East 140th Street: One-story classical bank with winged clock motif on facade. Extant (Mt. Pleasant Branch Library).
     Buckeye and East 89th Street: Designed February 1920. Elaborate building for a large irregular corner lot. Project aborted by Union Trust Company merger, December 1920. Unbuilt.

Broadway Savings and Trust Branches Designed December 1919.
     Broadway and East 55th Street: Major project for triangular eight-story stone-faced bank building with pilasters, a monumental arch at the corner entrance, and a central rotunda. Designer: C. W. Stedman. Unbuilt.
     Kinsman and East 140th Street: Branch bank combined with apartment units. Unbuilt. Both projects probably aborted by Union Trust Company merger, December 1920.

Warner & Swasey Observatory Taylor Road, East Cleveland, Ohio. Designed 1919. Astronomical observatory for Case School of Applied Science to house the telescope from the 1915 Panama-Pacific Exposition donated by Warner & Swasey Company. Long one-story building with two observatory domes and Lombardy Romanesque detail. Auditorium added 1940. Extant.

Edmund S. Burke Residence 11125 Magnolia Drive. Plans made in 1919 for alterations to the house originally designed by J. Milton Dyer in 1909. For the chairman of the Federal Reserve Bank of Cleveland. Extant (Cleveland Music School Settlement).

"Perspective Calculations" One folder in the Walker & Weeks collection is labeled "Perspective Calculations" and contains one or more perspective drawings

of thirteen projects for which they are the only visual record. The projects cover a large geographical area, and the majority are banks. Many, but not all, are dated 1919, which suggests that for a brief period the office was preoccupied with the mastery of perspective drawing. The projects are as follows:

Andover, Ohio	Andover Bank
Ansonia, Ohio	The Ansonia Building
Cleveland, Ohio	Industrial Association
Gallion, Ohio	Gallion Commercial Savings Bank
Hamilton, Ohio	First National Bank of Hamilton
Norwalk, Ohio	Citizens National Bank
Tiffin, Ohio	Tiffin National Bank
Angola, Illinois	First National Bank of Angola
Champaign, Ilinois	Champaign National Bank
Charleroi, Pennsylvania	First National Bank of Charleroi
Corry, Pennsylvania	National Bank of Corry
Erie, Pennsylvania	Erie Trust Company
Mt. Pleasant, Utah	Pleasant Commercial Savings Bank

Security Savings and Loan Company 710 Prospect Avenue. Designed January 1920. Interior marble details for a bank office in the existing Electric Building. Building extant.

Fort Recovery Bank Fort Recovery, Ohio. Designed January 1920. One-story bank with one large banking room. Drawings marked "Walker and Weeks, Bank Architects and Engineers." Extant.

Hotel and Bank Building for American National Bank Benton Harbor, Michigan. Designed January 1920. Seven-story hotel with bank offices on the first floor. Perspective sketch shows luxurious exterior. Not extant.

Hotel and Bank Building for Anderson Banking Company Anderson, Indiana. Designed February 1920. Eight-story hotel with three classical arches on facade, bank offices, cafeteria, and hotel lobby on the first floor.

Store and Professional Building for G. A. Ball Muncie, Indiana. Designed February 1920. Five-story building with display windows and retail space on first floor, and doctor's offices and private hospital-clinic on upper floors.

Broadway Savings and Trust, Broadway
Avenue at East 55th Street, 1919.

Bank and Office Building Unidentified. Preliminary study made in February 1920 for a twenty-story bank building connecting two streets, with lobbies at both ends and seven retail shops. Designer: C. W. Stedman. (See related design of Cleveland Discount Building, October 1920.)

James E. Ferris Residence 8910 Lake Shore Boulevard, Bratenahl. Designed February 1920. Interior design alterations and additions to an existing residence. Demolished.

Broadway Branch, Cleveland Public Library Mumford Avenue at East 55th Street. Designed February 1920. Small one-story branch library with an unusual sawtooth factory skylight roof. Unbuilt.

Federation Club Building Chester Avenue at East 13th Street. Designed March 1920. Proposed ten-story club building including welfare federation offices, recreation rooms, banquet rooms, Women's City Club and Men's City Club floors, attached to existing Benson parking garage on Dodge Court. Unbuilt. (See Women's City Club, 1922.)

Cleveland Discount Building 815–821 Superior Avenue NE. Designed October 1920. Twenty-story classical bank and office building with a narrow plan connecting Superior and Rockwell Avenues. Elaborate decorative details for elevator lobby and banking room with marble wainscoting, mosaic, and coffered ceilings. Extant (Superior Building). Altered.

Reliance Trust Company St. Clair Avenue and East 152nd Street. Designed August 1920. Alterations to an existing building including officers' rooms and new banking room details throughout. Not extant.

Marine National Bank Building Erie, Pennsylvania. Designed November 1920. Several versions were made 1920–22 for the alteration of a bank building including three retail stores and a large banking space.

Citizens Savings and Trust Euclid Avenue at East 101st Street. Designed 1920. Proposed major ten-story bank and office building with five bays on Euclid and eleven on East 101st. Unbuilt. Project aborted by Union Trust Company merger, December 1920.

Upson Nut Company Buildings Scranton and Carter Roads at Cleveland, Cincinnati, Chicago & St. Louis Railroad. Designed 1920. Extensive plans for several factory buildings, including a six-story structure of concrete column-and-slab construction with a monitor roof, and a one-story steel-framed building for shipping, packing, and offices. Extant.

Mount Union College Buildings Alliance, Ohio. Designed 1920. Various schemes for projected buildings were developed and revised through 1928, including a Memorial Gymnasium, concrete stadium bleachers, and a Library and Music

Conservatory in neoclassical and colonial styles. Gymnasium and stadium built. Extant.

Crispin Oglebay Outbuildings Gates Mills, Ohio. Undated. Probably ca. 1920. Plans for a riding stable, horse van and trailer garage, tool house, and interior details for the residence. Built for president of Oglebay Norton Company.

Playhouse Settlement Community Building Designed January 1921. Proposed community building for an East 38th Street site containing children's playrooms, lounges, gymnasium, and little theater. Planned for Russell and Rowena Jelliffe for the settlement that became Karamu House. Unbuilt.

Cleveland Athletic Club 1118 Euclid Avenue. Designed February 1921. Preliminary studies were made for a new ten-story building, with reference to plans by G. B. Post & Sons. Unbuilt. Also proposed additions to the existing building January 1929. Plans for remodeling the lobby and upper floors of the existing building May 1930 with interiors in the art moderne style. Extant.

First National Bank of Chardon Public Square Chardon, Ohio. Designed May 1921. Interior alterations to an existing nineteenth-century building, the Opera Block. Building extant.

Proposed Office Building Designed May 1921. Conceptual designs made for a twelve-, sixteen-, or twenty-one-story office building. Accompanying topographical survey suggests that the intended site was the southwest corner of Superior Avenue and West 6th Street. Designer: C. W. Stedman. Unbuilt.

Federal Reserve Bank East 6th Street at Superior. Designed September 1921. Major ten-story Renaissance-style building of granite and marble. Lavish interior decoration and ambitious symbolic sculptural program. Attributed to J. Byers Hays. Sculpture by Henry Hering. Extant.

Metropolitan Bank Building Undated. Proposed design for the site east of the Federal Reserve Bank on Superior Avenue. A neoclassic facade with a Roman arch and pilasters, and a ten-story annex adjacent to the Cleveland Discount Building. Unbuilt.

Sandusky Country Club at Lake Shore Electric Line, Sandusky, Ohio. Designed September 1921. One-and-a-half-story clubhouse with a steep gable roof, lounge and dining room, caretaker's quarters. In charge: Donald O. Dunn. Extant (Plum Brook Country Club, 3712 Galloway). Altered.

Erie County Bank Vermilion, Ohio. Designed September 1921. Alterations to a two-story brick bank building. Extant.

Peoples Banking Company Coshocton, Ohio. Designed November 1923. Small, narrow two-story bank building with offices. Unbuilt.

First National Bank of Greenville Main Street, Greenville, Pennsylvania. Designed November 1921. Extensive alterations and redesign for a bank building with a two-column in antis Ionic facade.

S. Prentiss Baldwin Residence 11025 East Boulevard. Designed 1921. Large stone mansion in the Renaissance style with a hip roof, porte-cochere, and a central hall, great living room, eleven bedrooms, servants' wing and attached garage. Demolished (Cleveland Institute of Music site).

George D. Harter Bank Market Street, Canton, Ohio. Designed 1921. Remarkable classical bank with a great Roman arch, garlanded frieze, and sculptured cartouche on the facade. Unusual interior with a wooden open-truss ceiling and skylight. Extant. Altered.

Building for Upper Euclid Company/Bamboo Gardens Euclid Avenue at East 100th Street. Designed 1921. Commercial building with six retail shops on the ground story, and restaurant and dance hall on the second. Decorative details for the restaurant in the Chinese style. Demolished.

Society National Bank Public Square. Designs 1921 for a proposed addition for the Safety Deposit Department on east side of building. Unbuilt. Designs 1928 and 1933–34 for alterations to banking room, changing John Wellborn Root's medieval design into a classical interior. Not executed.

Alliance Bank Building 504 East Main Street, Alliance, Ohio. Designed January 1922. Proposed additions to an existing six-story 1914 classical building for the Alliance Bank Company. Building extant.

Bank Building for Oglesby and Barnitz Company Main and Third Streets, Middletown, Ohio. Designed January 1922. Long, narrow bank with two-column in antis facade. Drawings marked "Walker & Weeks, Bank Architects and Engineers" and signed "Set approved by C. Byron Dalton."

Bank and Office Building for Reeves Realty Company West 3rd and Cherry Streets, Dover, Ohio. Designed January 1922. Three-story building with a four-bay facade of round arches. Extant.

Bank and Office Building for Harriman National Bank New York City. Designed March 1922. Proposed thirty-five-story office building with a ten-story base and a narrow setback tower to comply with New York zoning laws. Designer: C. W. Stedman. Unbuilt. Existing 535 Fifth Avenue building designed by H. Craig Severance.

Windsor Apartments Windsor Avenue and East 40th Street, Portland, Oregon. Designed April 1922. Large E-shaped apartment building with one-, two-, and three-bedroom apartments and two retail store spaces. Designer: C. W. Stedman. Status unknown.

Women's City Club 1826 East 13th Street. Designed May 1922. Two-story club building with reception and meeting rooms, dining room, cafeteria. Demolished.

Proposed Newcomer Apartments Designed June 1922. Proposed three-story luxury apartment building in the Georgian style between Nottinghill Lane and Cedar Road at the foot of Delamere, Cleveland Heights. Designer: J. Byers Hays. Reference to a similar plan by George B. Post & Sons. Unbuilt.

Athens National Bank Court Street, Athens, Ohio. Designed June 1922. Renovations to an existing five-story 1905 office building, occupied by Security Savings Bank in 1923. Extant.

First National Bank of Masillon 11 Lincoln Way West, Massillon, Ohio. Designed June 1922. Seven-story classical bank building with five bays on the side elevation. Extant.

Schwegler & Company Store Designed August 1922. Proposed four-story luxury interior decorating store in the Georgian colonial style. Planned for Euclid Avenue between East 70th and 71st Streets. Unbuilt.

National Bank of Commerce 457 Broadway, Lorain, Ohio. Designed October 1922. Alterations to an existing two-story classical building. Additional alterations 1929. Extant.

Dr. J. M. Ingersoll Residence Designed October 1922. This proposed residence was a complete restatement of the unbuilt Hellman house (1917). Like the Hellman house, the ill-fated design was built neither at the lot indicated on the plan, North Park Boulevard in Lot 422, nor at the client's actual address, 2218 Woodmere, Cleveland Heights. Landscape plan by A. D. Taylor.

Cleveland Life Insurance Building Euclid Avenue at East 31st Street. Designed 1922–23. Various schemes were made for an eight-story office building in neoclassic and Georgian styles, and a twenty-story version in the gothic style with art deco details. Unbuilt.

Francis E. Drury Estate SOM Center and Cedar Road, Gates Mills, Ohio. Plans made in 1922–26 for extensive formal gardens, a garden house, and an Italian Renaissance loggia on the estate. Main house (now Gilmour Academy) designed by Charles Schneider. Gardens not executed.

Howard M. Hanna Jr. Estate Stump Hollow Farm, Sperry Road, Kirtland, Ohio. Planned beginning ca. 1922. Extensive farm complex including farmhouse, horse barn, brick and fieldstone tenant houses in Greek revival and colonial styles, and ornamental arched stone bridges. Extant (Holden Arboretum).

J. A. Wigmore Cottage County Line Road, Chester Township, Geauga County, Ohio. Designed January 1923. Simple one-story U-shaped country house with servants' rooms in one wing and living rooms in the other.

Stockbridge Apartment 3328 Euclid Avenue. Designed February 1923. Four-story addition to the rear of an existing apartment building, with center corridor, single rooms with baths, and an elevator penthouse. Extant.

Proposed Office Building Philadelphia, Pennsylvania. Designed February 1923. Conceptual sketches were made for a fifteen-story office building with a classically arcaded penthouse and private officers' and directors' suites on the upper floors. Designer: C. W. Stedman. Status unknown.

Apartment Building for C. A. Ford Overlook Road, Cleveland Heights. Designed March 1923. Three-story apartment building planned in both Georgian and Adam styles. Unbuilt.

Home Bank and Trust Company Madison and Huron, Toledo, Ohio. Designed April 1923. Ten-story marble and limestone bank and office building with a ground-story Renaissance arcade and a bracketed cornice. Extant.

Mrs. Leonard C. Hanna Residence 10825 East Boulevard. Revisions May 1923 to masonry and stucco driveway gates and walls on a large property in the Wade Park Allotment. Extant.

Mrs. P. W. Harvey House Sincola Plantation, Pebble Hill, Thomasville, Georgia. Designed July 1923. Two-story colonial house flanked by a kitchen wing and a port-cochere. Included a matching dairyman's cottage and a colonial house of one-and-a-half stories. Status unknown.

H. M. Hanna Hunting Lodge Lake Miccassaukee, Florida, vicinity of Thomasville, Georgia. Undated.

C. F. Jackson Store West Main Street, Norwalk, Ohio. Designed August 1923. Proposed restoration of the 1893 "Glass Block" following a disastrous explosion, showing corner storefronts with slender iron columns and a great expanse of glass. Building extant. Altered.

City Savings Bank and Trust Company Main Street at Public Square, Alliance, Ohio. Designed August 1923. Preliminary conceptual drawings were made for enlarging an L-shaped 1917 building, giving the bank frontage on Main Street and Public Square, with two levels due to change in grade. Not extant.

Midland Bank Williamson Building, Euclid Avenue at Public Square. Designed August 1923. Plans for the banking room on the first floor of the Williamson Building. Midland Bank moved to the Terminal group in 1930. Williamson Building demolished.

First German Baptist Church Designed September 1923. Sketch plans and elevations for small one-story church and Sunday school in a simplified gothic style. Unbuilt.

El Pasadena Apartment St. Petersburg, Florida. Designed December 1923. Large four-story apartment building of Spanish colonial design with a splayed U-shape plan and a lobby leading to a circular domed glass solarium. The plans and elevations recall Hollywood settings. Unbuilt.

McKinney Steel Office Building 3100 East 45th Street. Designed December 1923. Four-story brick office building with a center corridor and offices. Extant (Cleveland District Plant, LTV Steel Company).

City Savings and Loan Williamson Building, Euclid Avenue at Public Square. Designed 1923. Alterations to a portion of the main floor of the Williamson Building for the City Savings and Loan Company. Williamson Building demolished.

Armen H. Tashjian Residence 2638 Fairmount Boulevard at Woodmere, Cleveland Heights. Designed 1923. Large residence with random ashlar walls, a half-timbered second story, massive hip roof, five bedrooms, servants' quarters and attached garage. For a partner in the Walker & Weeks firm. Extant.

St. Wendelin's Parish School and Chapel Designed before 1924. Three-story combination parochial school building and chapel. The planned site on Columbus Road and Freeman Avenue was bought by the Cleveland Union Terminals Company for the terminal approach. Extant church and school on Columbus Road and West 25th Street designed by William Dunn. Unbuilt.

Merchants Savings and Banking Company Huron Road and East 4th Street. Designed February 1924. Alterations and additions to an existing building, including a banking room, offices, and basement savings deposit vault. Demolished.

Lakewood Day Nursery 2070 Dowd Avenue, Lakewood, Ohio. Designed March 1924. Large two-story gable-roofed frame building of domestic character, with playrooms, dining room, dormitory, bedrooms, and babies' room. Extant.

Allen Memorial Medical Library 11000 Euclid Avenue. Designed March 1924. Major four-story Renaissance revival structure with a monumental stair lobby, library reading room and stacks, lounges, an auditorium, museum, and other facilities. Attributed to C. W. Stedman. Revisions made through 1927. Extant.

Euclid Avenue Baptist Church East 18th Street and Euclid Avenue. Designed April 1924. Major church in the Lombard Romanesque revival style, with fine brickwork and terra-cotta, a monumental tower, large auditorium sanctuary, and two-story Sunday school building. Attributed to J. Byers Hays. Demolished 1961.

Will R. Myers Residence 2935 Woodcliff Road, Canton, Ohio. Designed April 1924. The first plan was a restatement of the Nash house (1915). As built, it is more similar to the Judd residence. For secretary-treasurer, George D. Harter Bank, Canton. Extant. Avondale Development landscape design by Albert D. Taylor.

Proposed Residential Hotel Designed July 1924. Four-story "bachelors" hotel with retail shops, lounges, thirty-five rooms per floor, and a basement garage, designed for a site on Carnegie Avenue between East 105th and 106th Streets. Speculative plan for Frank J. Smith. Unbuilt.

University School Brantley and Claythorne Roads, Shaker Heights. Designed August 1924. Major complex including site planning, academic and administration building, dormitory, principal's residence, gymnasium, grandstand, and cottages, in the colonial revival style. Extant.

Petrequin Paper Company Office and Warehouse 1559 Superior Avenue. Designed September 1924. Long, narrow building between Superior and Rockwell Avenues, of reinforced concrete post-and-slab construction, with a classical stone facade. Extant.

United Banking and Trust Company West 25th Street and Lorain. Designed 1924. Nine-story bank and office building in the classical style, with a lavish baroque entrance on West 25th Street. Planned for expansion, but not executed. Extant.

Epworth-Euclid Methodist Church East 107th Street. Designed 1924. Bertram Goodhue, architect; Walker & Weeks, associated architects. Large modern gothic church with prominent central octagonal spire that dominates University Circle. Completed by Walker & Weeks after Goodhue's death. Extant.

Colonel Sam Tate Residence Tate, Pickens County, Georgia. Designed 1924. Large house and garage with floors of metal joists and concrete, and entirely faced with marble. For president of the Georgia Marble Company. Status unknown.

Proposed Medical Building Detroit, Michigan. Designed February 1925. Multistory medical building with basement garage, retail shops, waiting rooms, consulting suites, and operating room. Attributed to C. W. Stedman. Status unknown.

First National Bank Public Square, Youngstown, Ohio. Designed May 1925. Twelve-story classical bank and office building with an entrance of two giant Corinthian columns in antis and a secondary pedimented building entrance. Extant.

Peoples Trust Company Lancaster, Pennsylvania. Designed August 1925. Alterations and additions to an existing 1887 bank building in the Romanesque style, converting it to a Doric order classical building. Attributed to Dana Clark. Status unknown.

Old National City Building 121 West High Street, Lima, Ohio. Designed October 1925. Major fourteen-story modernistic skyscraper office and bank building with strong vertical piers and an arched entrance. Banking hall with vaulted ceiling and windows. Includes alterations in 1935 and 1939. Extant.

Cleveland Museum of Natural History East Boulevard. Designed 1925. A proposed beaux-arts classical design for the museum at University Circle. A two-story, 3.5 million cubic foot building. Planetarium projected 1931 in consultation with German optical experts. Unbuilt.

Sterling and Welch Warehouse Chester Avenue between East 12th and East 13th Streets. Designed 1925. Additions and alterations to the service structure for the store on Euclid Avenue by J. Milton Dyer. Demolished.

Sarasota Race Track Sarasota, Florida. Designed 1925. Site plans for a one-mile race track, 4,000-seat grandstand, stables, boarding house, jockey clubhouse, members' club house, and two-story circular Day Clubs. Notes for the building program include names of John Ringling North, Price McKinney, and A. D. Taylor, landscape architect. Unbuilt.

Halle Brothers Company New Building Huron Road–Prospect Avenue. Designed January 1926. Large six-story department store annex designed to harmonize with the original 1910 Euclid Avenue terra-cotta building by Henry Bacon. Included designs for a proposed bridge over Huron Road in both Venetian Palladian and art deco styles. Attributed to Dana Clark. Building extant. Bridge unbuilt.

Presbyterian Church Wooster, Ohio. Designed January 1926. Proposed stone gothic sanctuary and Sunday school building. The church was finally built to plans by J. C. Fulton, Uniontown, Pennsylvania.

Ohio Bell Telephone Morningside Office Kinsman Avenue at East 158th Street, Shaker Heights. Designed February 1926. Two-story concrete-frame, brick-faced, apparatus and operator building in the Georgian style, meeting Shaker Heights design standards. Later Washington Branch. Extant. Altered. Third story added.

Coca Cola Company Office Building Plum Street, Atlanta, Georgia. Designed March 1926. Additions and alterations to the Coca Cola headquarters building for executive, advertising, and display departments. Original 1920 building by Hentz, Reid & Adler, with Philip Shutze, associated architects. Demolished.

Hathaway-Brown School 19600 North Park Boulevard, Shaker Heights, Ohio. Designed May 1926. Campus plan and buildings in the English Tudor style for private girls' school. Main classroom building and separate dormitory building. Reference made to the old Hathaway-Brown building at 1945 East 97th Street, Cleveland. Extant.

Smith and Gerhart Store Building 520 Broadway, Lorain, Ohio. Designed May 1926. Three-story addition to an existing store building, with a facade of fluted pilasters and a concrete frame. Extant. Altered.

Indiana World War Memorial Memorial Plaza, Indianapolis, Indiana. Designed June 1926. Complete design for a five-block-long, 500-foot-wide memorial plaza with four major buildings, cenotaph, fountain square, and an obelisk. The main shrine is a 195-foot-tall memorial structure. Design source the Mausoleum of Halicarnassus, with a pyramidal roof and forty-five-foot Ionic colonnades. Design attributed to J. Byers Hays. The firm was involved in the project for twenty years. Included the American Legion National Headquarters and Auxiliary buildings on the plaza, 1945. Proposed Headquarters for the Department of Indiana and for *La Societe des Quarante Hommes et Huit Chevaux*, 1945. Extant.

Weisberger Company Store Barberton, Ohio. Designed July 1926. Three-story department store with a brick facade and five arched window bays, storefront display window islands at the entrance, and interior salesroom with counters. Unbuilt.

Bellefontaine Building and Loan Company Bellefontaine, Ohio. Designed July 1926. Two-story savings and office building with an arched classical facade, a small public banking room, vault and working space, and second-story offices including layout for doctors' rooms. Extant.

Professional Building for James D. Shipton School and North Streets, Pittsfield, Massachusetts. Designed September 1926. Six-story office building with a drugstore and two retail stores on the street floor, and doctors' offices, reception, consulting, treatment, and operating rooms on upper floors. Attributed to C. W. Stedman. Extant.

Merchants National Bank Hillsboro, Ohio. Designed November 1926. New facade design with classical pilasters for an existing two-story bank building with a nineteenth-century subsidewalk areaway, banking room and one retail store. Unbuilt.

Apartment Building for Lee-More Company Lee Road and Van Aken (old South Moreland) Boulevard, Shaker Heights, Ohio. Designed November 1926. Three-story L-shaped commercial, office, and apartment building in the Tudor style, with brick facing, half-timbering, and gothic details. Extant. Also made plans for Lee-More for a commercial building at Broadway and Miles Road.

2341 Carnegie Building Designed December 1926. Six-story office building with a classical facade which contained Walker & Weeks's own offices and large drafting room with clerestory, occupying the fifth and sixth floors. Automotive showroom on the ground floor. Extant.

Hollenden Hotel Superior Avenue and East 6th Street. Designed 1926. $5 million expansion of the existing 1885 chateau-style hotel, including modernization of the south section and the addition of a ten-story east wing in the Georgian style. Demolished.

Greater Wesleyan College Macon, Georgia. Designed 1926. Campus plans for a Methodist women's college, consisting of six linked two-story brick buildings in a simplified colonial style, with marble-columned verandas. Dunwoody & Oliphant, associated architects. Extant.

Federal Reserve Bank of Cleveland Cincinnati Branch, Fourth and Race Streets, Cincinnati, Ohio. Designed 1926. Plans for the branch Federal Reserve Bank located in the fourteen-story Chamber of Commerce building, Tietig & Lee and Hake and Kuck, architects, Cincinnati. Edwin J. Truthan in charge. Building extant.

Towell Cadillac Building East 30th Street at Chester Avenue. Designed 1926. Addition of a third story to an existing 1916 automotive building of yellow brick with terra-cotta arches. Also proposed an alternate scheme for a new building in the modernistic style. Extant.

Cleveland Public Library Branches Designed 1926–27.
   Glenville, 660 Parkwood Drive.
   Harvey Rice, 2820 East 116th Street.
   Collinwood, 856 East 152nd Street, modernized classic design with a large arched center entrance.
   East 131st Branch, 3830 East 131st Street, similar design with the entrance enlarged to an arched vestibule. Notable glazed terra-cotta ornament.
   West Park Branch, 3805 West 157th Street, similar in plan but with a steep gabled roof and Tudor revival detail to harmonize with a residential section.
   All branches extant.

Wolfe Music Store 2112 Euclid Avenue. Erected 1927. A three-story store building with a marble and bronze-framed store front and delicately ornamented terra-cotta facade and pediment. Extant.

William J. Hunkin Residence 17710 Shaker Boulevard, Shaker Heights, Ohio. Designs February 1927 for interior details of library. House probably built 1923. For the founder of Hunkin-Conkey Construction Company. Extant.

St. Paul's Episcopal Church 2747 Fairmount Boulevard, Cleveland Heights, Ohio. Designed June 1927. A large church of stone construction in a simplified English gothic revival idiom. Parish hall and tower were built in 1928–29. Design altered for main sanctuary in 1949–51. Designer: J. Byers Hays. Extant.

John C. Lowe Residence 2357 Tudor Drive, Cleveland Heights. Designs July 1927 for remodeling interior details and woodwork. Originally built for president of John C. Lowe Company, makers of umbrellas and canes. House occupied by Harry Weeks in 1928. Extant.

Proposed Lincoln at Gettysburg Statue Euclid Avenue at East 14th Street. Designed July 1927. Stepped plaza and pedestal for a statue of Lincoln by Max Kalish. Attributed to Dana Clark. Unbuilt. Statue was eventually erected at Board of Education Headquarters in 1930.

Broadview Baptist Church Designed July 1927. Proposed new structure in the

Georgian revival style for the church at 4505 Broadview Road. Unbuilt.

Pearl Street Savings and Trust West 25th Street at Clark Avenue. Designed September 1927. Four-story office and bank building. Unusually complete documentation exists for the evolution of the design from a neoclassic scheme with a large facade arch to the final modernistic design with art deco pilasters and ornament. Vaulted banking-room ceiling. Attributed to Dana Clark. Extant.

Western Reserve University Law School Designed October 1927. A two-story T-shaped academic building with a large assembly hall, lecture halls, law library, and faculty offices. Attributed to C. W. Stedman. Unbuilt.

Cleveland School of Art East Boulevard at Bellflower Road. Designed November 1927. Conjectural diagrams of a proposed site for the art school building, consisting of studios, administrative offices, lecture hall, library, and other facilities. Unusual angled U-shape plan. Attributed to C. W. Stedman. Unbuilt.

Masonic Temple 38117 Euclid Avenue, Willoughby, Ohio. Designed 1927. Irregular five-sided three-story building with two stores, lodge hall, auditorium, lounge and banquet hall. Proposed facade elevations were made in two versions, one brick and stone, the other all stone with art deco pilasters. Extant.

Church of Christ Willoughby, Ohio. Designed 1927. A proposed sanctuary with classical revival and Georgian detail. Unbuilt.

St. Christopher's-by-the-River Old Mill Road, Gates Mills, Ohio. Designed 1927. Restoration, moving of social hall, and addition of a chancel to a nineteenth-century Greek revival church. Designer: Frank Walker. Extant.

37th Division Memorial Bridge River Scheldt, L'Escaut a Eyne, Belgium. Competition design 1927. A 121-foot (37 meter) slender arched span erected as World War I memorial by the 37th Division Battle Memorial Commission of the State of Ohio. Existing diagrams of concrete (beton) reinforcing for the span, foundations, and retaining walls are in French. Destroyed in World War II. Reconstructed 1950. Replaced 1980.

World War Memorial Competition Designs Montfaucon and Hattonchatel, France. Designed 1927. Competition entries for a stone tower with an allegorical figure and a clock for Montfaucon; and a rectangular stone gateway with fluted piers and a symbolic eagle for Hattonchatel. Neither design awarded or built.

St. Ann's Parish Church Cleveland Heights. Original designs 1927–28. (See St. Ann's Parish Church, 1945.)

The Columbus Memorial Lighthouse Competition Designed 1927–29. Entry for a major international competition for a lighthouse memorial to Christopher Columbus in the Dominican Republic. A fantastic art deco monument with

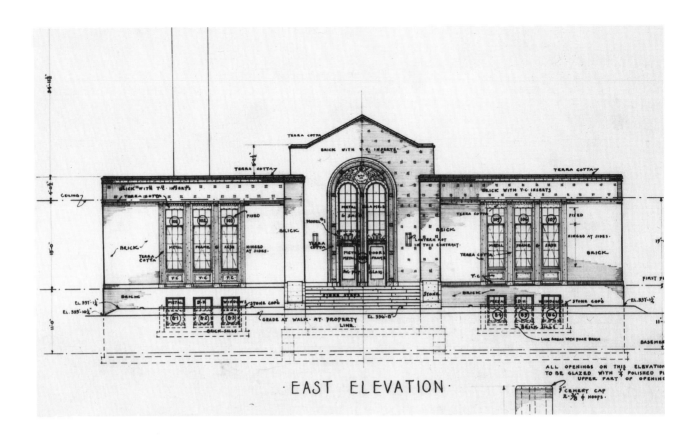

·EAST ELEVATION·

East 131st Street Branch, Cleveland Public Library, 1928.

three colossal pylons adorned with sculptured pre-Columbian American ornament. Color renderings were executed in the style of Hollywood settings. Competition entry neither awarded nor built.

Proposed Office Building for Southern Railway, Pennsylvania Avenue and 12th Street NW, Washington, D.C. Designed February 1928. Five-story commercial and office building with thirty retail units and open-plan upper floors. Attributed to Edwin J. Truthan. Unbuilt. Extant Southern Railway Building at 15th and "K" Streets designed by Waddy Butler Wood, Washington, D.C.

Caxton Building 812 Huron Road. Designs March 1928 for additions and alterations to the existing 1903 building by Coburn and Barnum, remodeling the entrance lobby and street fronts. Building extant.

H. W. Strong Residence 2225 Delamere Road, Cleveland Heights. Designs April 1928 for addition of a two-story curved bay to the rear elevation of an existing house, possibly designed by Walker & Weeks. Extant.

West Park Branch, Cleveland Public
Library, 1927.

Peoples Trust and Savings Bank Fort Wayne, Indiana. Designed May 2928. Interior alterations to an existing six-story building with a facade of four mannerist segmented columns. Original building by Charles P. Weatherhogg, Fort Wayne.

L. B. Walters Residence Riverside Drive, Painesville, Ohio. Designed May 1928. Addition of two rooms to an existing house, making a five-bay colonial facade with an elaborate Adamesque entrance and sidelights. For president of Painesville National Bank. Extant.

William H. Hunt Residence Hemlock Road, Independence, Ohio. Designed June 1928. Proposal for a fantastic eclectic shingled mansion with a gothic porte-cochere and central octagonal tower. Site developed with a series of promenade terraces stepping down to the Cuyahoga Valley. Designed for president of Cleveland Life Insurance Company. House unbuilt. Terraces extant.

One of two very different designs for the Willoughby Masonic Temple, 1927.

Proposed Parish Church for Episcopal Diocese of Ohio Designed June 1928. Small English gothic sanctuary. Not identified as a specific parish or as a generic parish church.

Capital National Bank Capital and Allegan Streets, Lansing, Michigan. Designed August 1928. A seventeen-story setback office tower with main hall banking room on the first floor. Various massing schemes were made for the tower: rectangular modernistic, classic colonnade, and topped with a pyramid.

Lincoln National Bank and Trust Company 116–122 Berry Street, Fort Wayne, Indiana. Designed August 1928–30. A major twenty-two-story setback skyscraper in the modernistic style, with strong vertical piers, lavish art deco ornament on the lower stories, and a lobby with ornamental plaster columns. A. M. Strauss, associated architect. Extant.

Clinic Hospital Lima Locomotive Works, Lima, Ohio. Designed September 1928. Three-story company hospital building with treatment rooms, surgery, and two floors of patient rooms. Extant.

First Church of Christ, Scientist Overlook Road, Cleveland Heights, Ohio. Designed September 1928. Octagonal sanctuary with a tall campanile in the transitional classical-modern style. Attributed to Dana Clark. An earlier version for a Euclid Avenue site with a low Roman dome was the prototype for Severance Hall. Extant.

Building and Loan Company Wooster, Ohio. Designed December 1928. A nine-story office building with vertical piers and ornamental spandrels in the modernistic style. Unbuilt.

First Baptist Church Fairmount Boulevard at Eaton Road, Shaker Heights, Ohio. Designed 1928. A large simplified modern gothic church with a square tower and a large Sunday school unit. The design is related to that of St. Paul's Episcopal Church. Attributed to J. Byers Hays. Extant.

Commercial National Bank Coshocton, Ohio. Designed 1928. Alterations to roof, vault, and interiors of an existing bank building. Demolished.

A. C. Ernst Estate Chagrin River Road, Gates Mills, Ohio. Designs 1928–41 for a three-story colonial house with a center block and flanking wings for servants and a conservatory, a Dutch farmhouse garage and maid's quarters, pony barn with symmetrical wings, and alterations to a small one-and-a-half-story Greek revival-style house. Extant.

Ohio Wesleyan College Delaware, Ohio. Designed 1928–38. Consultants to the university and master plans for the campus 1928–38. Consulting architects on Selby Field, an athletic stadium with two concrete stands, erected 1928 by Osborn Engineering Company. Extant. Women's campus including a three-story U-shaped dormitory in the Georgian style for 200 women, 1930; actually built from plans by Warner and Mitchell. Alterations to existing 1856 Sturges Hall, 1938.

Cleveland Municipal (Lakefront) Stadium Final designs January 1929. Osborn Engineering Company, with Walker & Weeks, associate architects. A great oval multipurpose stadium with brick walls, aluminum superstructure, and four masonry towers. C. W. Stedman in charge. Demolished.

Hotel and Theater Building Designed January 1929 for a site at West 3rd Street and Superior Avenue. A fourteen-story office or hotel tower combined with a 1,645-seat theater, bowling alley, and stores. For Frank Johnson. Unbuilt.

Medical Center Building West Market and Cherry Streets, Akron, Ohio. Designed January 1929. Proposed complex on an irregular five-sided lot, with reception, consulting, operating, and other medical facilities, plus a three-level parking garage. Unbuilt.

Central Savings and Trust Building 106 South Main Street, Akron, Ohio. Designed February 1929. Major twenty-seven-story modernistic skyscraper office tower. Studies were made for the zoning envelope and building massing. Art deco lobby and elevators and lavish floral-geometric ornament for main entrance. Attributed to C. W. Stedman. Extant.

Hotel Delmont Canton, Ohio. Designed March 1929. A thirteen-story hotel building with ground-floor commercial facilities. Attributed to C. W. Stedman. Designed for Francis A. Onesto. Extant Hotel Onesto at North Market and Second Streets NW designed by J. C. Stevenson of H. L. Stevens Company, Chicago.

Searles Motor Company 14401–14447 Euclid Avenue, East Cleveland, Ohio. Designed March 1929. One-story automobile sales building with showroom, service, and parts areas. Facade with plate-glass show windows, face brick, and stone detail. For Mabel Minshall and John A. Cline. Demolished.

New York Central and Nickel Plate Railroad Bridges Euclid Avenue, Mayfield Road, Cedar Glen, and East Boulevard. Designed April 1929. Heavy steel girder bridges with modernistic ornamental detail on the concrete and sandstone piers. Extant.

Niles Trust Company Main and Park Streets, Niles, Ohio. Designed April 1929. Six-story modernistic building with vertical piers, a penthouse, and interior banking room elevation with characteristic zigzag ornament. William E. Becker and Byron Dalton in charge. Extant.

Gail S. Grant Company 165 Main Street, Painesville, Ohio. Designed May 1929. Remodeling of an existing building with new basement stairs and floor framing.

Morris Plan Bank and Office Building Evansville, Indiana. Designed June 1929. McGuire & Shook, architects, with Walker & Weeks, associated architects. An eight-story office building in the modernistic style, with an eight-bay facade, geometric vertical piers, and spandrel ornament.

Henry A. Taylor Residence 1251 Oakridge Drive, Cleveland Heights. Designed July 1929. A two-and-a-half-story gable-front and wing residence in a Greek revival style, with stone veneer on the first story and clapboard above. Sloping site gives additional level to the rear. Extant.

Central National Bank Battle Creek, Michigan. Designed December 1929. A twenty-story modernistic skyscraper office and bank building. Various schemes included one with a fifty-car garage and a grand stairwell from the entrance lobby to the second-level banking room. Designer: C. W. Stedman.

Lorain-Carnegie (Central, Hope Memorial) Bridge Cuyahoga River Valley connecting Lorain and Carnegie Avenues. Designed 1929. Engineering design by Wilbur Watson. Architectural design by Walker & Weeks. High-level bridge spanning the Cuyahoga, with thirteen cantilever truss spans. Four sculptured pylons representing Guardians of Traffic designed by Walker and sculptured by Henry Hering. Also designed were unbuilt approaches at both ends. Extant.

Schulte United Department Store 520 Euclid Avenue. Designed 1929. Alterations to an existing 1887 building, with a new five-story, five-bay facade with vertical fluted piers and spandrel ornament in the modernistic style. Contains the Euclid Avenue entrance to the Colonial Arcade. Extant.

Halle Brothers Store 624 North Market Street, Canton, Ohio. Designed 1929. A two-story branch department store building. Later Polsky's. Extant. Altered.

William Taylor Son & Company Designed 1929. Proposed high-rise setback skyscraper department store building at the 630 Euclid Avenue/Prospect Avenue site. Unbuilt. Renderings by Wilbur Adams in the Hugh Ferriss manner. Walker & Weeks also planned alterations to the existing store.

Severance Hall Euclid Avenue at East Boulevard. Designed 1929–30. The concert hall of the Cleveland Orchestra, a major building in a transitional classical-modernistic style. Polygonal mass with a temple-front portico, and an interior with art deco detail and color including a delicate floral ceiling pattern in the "French modernistic" style. Innovative color organ planned by S. R. MacCandless and Dean Holden. Extant.

State Life Insurance Building Indianapolis, Indiana. Undated. Large three-story office building containing offices, open-plan upper floors, meeting hall, and two inner courts. An earlier scheme shows Corinthian columns that were changed to a facade with modernistic vertical piers and ornamental spandrels. Draftsman: F.L.W. Unbuilt.

American Trust and Savings Bank Evansville, Indiana. Designed March 1930. Thole & Legeman, associated architects. Classical alterations to an existing four-story office building, including a proposed addition of two stories. Preliminary scheme was dated September 1929.

East 18th–Euclid Building 1739 Euclid Avenue. Designed March 1930. Proposed alterations to the existing two-story Guenther Building (1915), either to alter the classical facade or to add six stories in the gothic style. Attributed to C. W. Stedman.

Lotus Garden Restaurant designed for the second story in the modernistic style with Chinese decoration, notable for a "Colorama" changing interior lighting system. 1930.

Also remodeled the building for the *Builders Exchange* 1941. Building extant. Altered (Cleveland State University).

Administration Building, Cleveland Board of Education 1380 East 6th Street. Designed May 1930. Six-story E-shaped office building with two main entrances facing East 6th Street and the Mall. A center-corridor plan with offices and meeting rooms. Designed to conform with the Group Plan requirements for the Mall buildings, with rusticated basement, arched entrances, and classical detail. Extant.

Oberlin College Swimming Pool Oberlin, Ohio. Designed July 1930. College building containing pool, locker rooms, and game rooms. Five variant schemes were made, all consistent with the campus style set by Cass Gilbert, with Romanesque arches and tiled hip roofs. Designer: C. W. Stedman. Extant (Crane Pool).

Schofield Building Euclid Avenue at East 9th Street. Designs October 1930 for alterations in the modernistic style to the entrance and ground-story facades of the existing thirteen-story office building (1901) by Levi Scofield [*sic*].

Also alterations November 1940 for penthouse and elevator reconditioning. Extant. Altered.

Guerdon S. Holden Residence 9511 Lake Shore Boulevard, Bratenahl, Ohio. Designed November 1930. Remodeling of library and living room of an existing house. For the son of Liberty Holden and a director of Forest City Publishing, publishers of the *Plain Dealer*. Extant.

Federal Reserve Bank of Cleveland, Pittsburgh Branch Grant Street and Ogle Way, Pittsburgh, Pennsylvania. Designed November 1930. An eight-story building in the modernistic style with a facade of three center bays and vertical piers of marble. Notable for use of exterior architectural metal. Edwin J. Truthan in charge. Wood and Hornbostel, Pittsburgh, consulting architects. Extant.

Bucks County Courthouse Doylestown, Pennsylvania. Designed 1930. A proposed four-story modernistic government building with rectangular piers and geometric art deco spandrels. Unbuilt.

Father Jacques Marquette Memorial Gary, Indiana. Designed January 1931. Pedestal and site plan for a bronze statue of the seventeenth-century French Jesuit priest. Extant. (See Gary Civic Center, 1932.)

Evansville Public Library SE Fifth Street and Locust Street, Evansville, Indiana. Designed 1930. Harry E. Boyle & Company, Evansville, associated architects. Four-story library with reading rooms, stacks, and various departmental rooms. Seven-bay stone-faced facade having metal-framed bay windows and cast ornament.

Central United National Bank 1612 Euclid Avenue. Designed March 1931. Classical alterations to an existing nineteenth-century building. Demolished.

Ball Building 1114 Euclid Avenue. Planned April 1931. Renovation of an existing nineteenth-century store building for Webb C. Ball, jewelers. Victorian facade of projecting bay windows replaced with art deco piers and spandrels. Extant.

Main Avenue Bridge Cuyahoga River Valley, connecting Bulkley Boulevard and West 3rd Street. Numerous sketch plans of various bridge designs were made between April 1931 and September 1932. Multiple-arch steel spans, with stone pylons and a traffic control station at the West 28th Street end. Existing 1939 Main Avenue Bridge designed by Wilbur Watson.

Guardian Trust and Savings Branch 10300 Euclid Avenue. Designed September 1931. Alterations to an existing building, first occupied by Guardian Trust in 1922. Demolished.

Goodyear Service Station Chester Avenue and East 13th Street. Designed October 1931. Automobile service station with strong horizontal lines in the art moderne or international style idiom, with dramatic vertical sign pylons. Attributed to Wilbur H. Adams. Demolished.

Warner Bateman Reo Automobile Salesroom Carnegie Avenue and East 83rd Street. Designed November 1931. Automobile sales building with showroom, service garage, and used car lot. Modern-style facade with vertical pylon sign, black tile, and opal glass. Revised version designed May 1933. Unbuilt.

George W. Merz Residence 424 North Portage Path, Akron, Ohio. Designed 1931. Eclectic residence with a gothic entry, vertical rectangular tower, and half-timbering. Designer: Charles H. Stark II. Extant.

Harrison County Courthouse Clarksburg, West Virginia. Designed 1931. Six-story modernistic office building of granite and limestone with vertical piers and decorative metal. Sculptured eagles by Henry Hering flank the entrance. Interiors with art deco detail and furnishings. Carleton C. Wood, Clarksburg, associated architect. Extant.

Civic Center, Museum and Monument Gary, Indiana. Designed April 1932. Site plans for Gateway Park Civic Center; Historical Museum with colossal Statue of Vulcan; Washington Monument in Washington Park. Museum consisted of three linked shapes—rectangular, circular, and trapezoidal—to house museums of steel, the history of Gary, and metals. Unbuilt.

Toledo Trust Company Superior and Madison Avenues, Toledo, Ohio. Designed 1932. Alterations to the existing 1916 classical bank building by Mills, Rhines, Bellman & Nordhoff. Extant.

United States Post Office Prospect Avenue. Designed 1932. Walker & Weeks and Philip L. Small & Associates, associated architects. Monumental five-story government building of modernistic design, with fluted vertical piers between each rank of windows. Erected on air rights of Cleveland Union Terminals Company property. Extant. Original sandstone facing replaced with precast panels in 1979.

Frank H. Ginn Estate Old Mill Road, Gates Mills, Ohio. Designed January 1933. Alterations to the interior of an existing country house. Drawings signed by F.R.W. and D.C. (Clark). Plans for a gardener's single cottage and a two-story double cottage, August 1936. For prominent lawyer with Tolles, Hogsett, Ginn & Morley.

Lincoln Statue Pedestal Lincoln Memorial Bridge, Milwaukee, Wisconsin. Designed April 1933. Sketch plans for pedestal in the form of an armchair. Attributed Clark. Sculpture by Henry Hering.

Edison Memorial Bridge Route 39 (old) at the Huron River, Milan, Ohio. Designed May 1933. Ambitious proposed bridge crossing the Huron River valley on the axis of the main street in Milan. Six-span concrete-arch structure with an illuminated memorial shaft to Thomas Edison at one end. Unbuilt.

Building at 2032 Euclid Avenue Designed October 1933. Renovations to an existing building, replacing one storefront bay with an overhead door for Reed's Auto Service. Planned for Evan Hopkins. Demolished.

Gallipolis Locks and Dam Ohio River at Eureka, Ohio. Designed 1933–34. Walker was architectural consultant to the U.S. Government on the project including the Gallipolis roller dam, with eight 130-foot piers at 125-foot intervals, and three dams on the Kanawaha River in West Virginia at Marmet, London, and Winfield. Extant.

Citizens National Bank Perrysburg, Ohio. Designed January 1934. Small one-story center hall bank building with a three-bay brick facade in the colonial style and an entrance framed by an arch. Unbuilt.

Reid Avenue Underpass Nickel Plate Railroad, Lorain, Ohio. Designed 1934. Railroad bridge of heavy steel girders and concrete abutments. Unbuilt.

Carter Hotel 1020 Prospect Avenue. Designed 1934. Remodeling of the existing Winton Hotel (1917) for the Albert Pick Company. Associated with Welch-Wilmarth Designing for interiors. Extant. Altered.

Secor Hotel 425 Jefferson Street, Toledo, Ohio. Designed 1934. Remodeling of the existing hotel building (1908) for the Albert Pick Company. Extant. Altered.

Cleveland Clinic Memorial Auditorium Designed May 1935 for proposed Memorial Hall and Museum, containing a lecture hall seating 694, meeting rooms, and a 110-car garage. Designers: Stedman and Clark. Unbuilt.

Republic Building 643 Euclid Avenue. Designed 1935. Alterations to an existing building for the Blue Boar Restaurant. Demolished.

McDowell National Bank Sharon, Pennsylvania. Designed 1935. Alterations of interiors, details, and mechanical systems for an existing bank building.

Jefferson County Courthouse Steubenville, Ohio. Designed ca. 1935. Proposed four-story modernistic government building with rectangular fluted piers and art deco ornament. Unbuilt.

Charles H. Strong Estate Tuckaway Farm, Kirtland-Chardon Road, Kirtland, Ohio. Designed 1935–41. Extensive alterations to an existing residence with the

Bucks County Courthouse, Doylestown,
Pennsylvania, 1930.

addition of a new living room–bedroom wing. Draftsman: F.R.W. For the president of William Taylor Son & Company.

Great Lakes Exposition Cleveland lakefront. Designed 1935–36. Walker & Weeks designed the bridge across the railroad tracks to the lakefront exhibition area, ornamented with fourteen stylized sculptured eagles. Also plans for East 9th Street underpass; the Leisy Casino, a fanciful wooden building of three linked octagonal pagodalike structures; and a temple pavilion for the Model Garden of the Gates Mills Garden Club. Designer: Dana Clark. Temporary structures. Dismantled.

Engel and Fetzer Store 1228 Huron Road. Designed March 1936. Alterations to an existing retail store building with interior details and a fur storge vault. Extant. Altered.

James L. Luke Residence Burke Estate, Kinsman Road, Russell Township, Geauga County, Ohio. Designed May 1936. Large two-story residence in a free Georgian idiom. For treasurer, Cleveland-Cliffs Iron Company. Attributed to Dana Clark. Unbuilt.

Protected Home Circle Building Sharon, Pennsylvania. Designed May 1936. A four-story irregular-plan office building in the modernistic style, with retail spaces, business offices, executive offices, and lodge meeting room. Exterior with vertical piers and a central setback entrance tower.

Mayer-Marks Company Store Designed August 1936. A modernistic facade of multicolored tile or architectural glass applied to an existing building, probably

Civic Center, museum and monument,
Gary, Indiana, 1933, plan of museum.

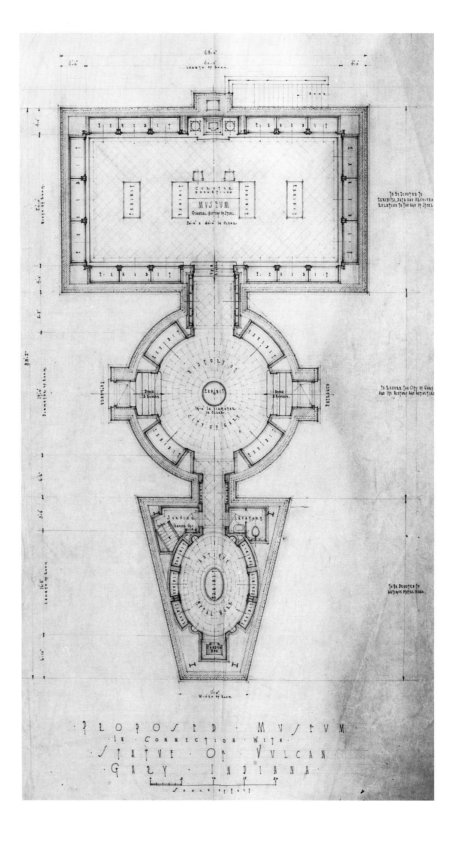

the 1903 building of the company's main store at 414 Prospect Avenue. Attributed to Dana Clark. Not extant.

Farmers Deposit National Bank Fifth and Wood Streets, Pittsburgh, Pennsylvania. Designed September 1936. Addition of a safe-deposit department and vault to an existing commercial bank. Design included a mural with Roman figures in glass, copper, bronze, and Allegheny metal. Building extant. Altered.

Ellastone Building 408 Prospect Avenue. Designed October 1936. Alterations to an existing building. Demolished.

Dudley A. Hawley Residence, Mitchell Mills Road, Chardon Township, Geauga County, Ohio. Designed October 1936. Small one-story country house with living room, kitchen, bath, and a six-bed dormitory.

H. M. Hanna Tenant House Stump Hollow Farm, Sperry Road, Kirtland, Ohio. Designed November 1936. A small house in the Greek revival style, with studs, rafters, and windows framed in steel by Stran Steel Corporation and Detroit Steel Products, Detroit. In charge: Dana Clark. Extant (Holden Arboretum).

William C. Scott Residence 5992 Darrow Road, Hudson, Ohio. Designed 1936. A stone-faced classical revival residence. In charge: C. W. Stedman. For secretary and counsel M. A. Hanna Company. Extant.

Kinsman (Mount Pleasant), Superior, and South Brooklyn Branches, Cleveland Public Library Designed 1936. Alterations to existing building at 13512 Kinsman. Additions to existing Superior branch at 1347 East 105th Street. Designer: C. W. Stedman. Alterations to existing Union Trust Bank at Pearl Road and Henritze for South Brooklyn Branch Library. All buildings extant.

Noble Road Branch Library 2800 Noble Road, Cleveland Heights. Erected 1937. A Georgian colonial suburban library with a gable-end facade, pedimented entrance, and side wings. Extant.

Walter T. Kinder Residence Carpenter Road at Old Mill Road, Gates Mills. Designed April 1937. Alterations and additions to the front portico, rear porch, library, windows, and interior details on an existing house. Extant.

St. Lawrence Catholic Church East 81st Street. Designed April 1937. Church in the Lombard Romanesque revival style, with prominent campanile. The existing basement phase was built in 1924. Completed church (1940) attributed to George Voinovich, who left Walker & Weeks 1939. Extant.

English Lutheran Church Undated. Sketch plans for a church in the Romanesque revival style, similar in design to St. Lawrence Church. Drawings by F.R.W. and D. Clark.

Glen Arven Country Club Thomasville, Georgia. Designed May 1937. A T-shaped club building and swimming pool in a simplified colonial style. Inscription for a Howard M. Hanna Memorial in the pool room. Extant.

Statler Hotel Alterations Euclid Avenue at East 12th Street. Designed May 1937 and later for alterations to the lobby, street shops, dining room, and ballroom, with some facade work. Original design by George B. Post & Sons. Building extant (Statler Office Tower). Altered.

Bailey Company Store Building Designed June 1937. Large branch department store building with three smaller retail spaces planned for the corner of Euclid Avenue and East 107th Street. Attributed to C. W. Stedman. Unbuilt.

H. P. Forker Jr. Estate 422 East State Street, Sharon, Pennsylvania. Designed June 1937. Plans for an ornamental wall and driveway layout.

Ford Building Griswold and Congress Streets, Detroit, Michigan. Designed October 1937. Plans for modernizing the lower three stories of the 1909 building by D. H. Burnham and Company. Attributed to Dana Clark. Extant.

Office Building for Anthony Carlin 1326 Huron Road at East 14th Street. Designed October 1937. Proposed theater and office building. Reference plans for TransLux theaters in New York by Thomas Lamb and Walker & Gillette. Attributed to Stedman. Planned for president of Anthony Carlin Company, rivet manufacturers. Theater unbuilt. Two-story retail building erected. Demolished.

Lorain County Courthouse Elyria, Ohio. Recommendations 1937 for alterations to the existing nineteenth-century Renaissance revival building, including the removal of the cupola. Extant.

Medina Theater Medina, Ohio. Designed 1937. Picture theater planned for the Public Square. Unbuilt.

Chemical Engineering Building Case School of Applied Science. Designed April 1938. Three-story science building with office, classroom, and laboratory spaces. Exterior design with strongly pronounced horizontal brick banding and modernistic style entrance way. Extant (Albert W. Smith Building). Altered.

Medina Hospital Designed May 1938. Proposed scheme for an ideal small hospital building, with three curved decks in the art moderne idiom and a geometric setback entrance block. Drawings by Dana Clark.

Geneva Hospital drawings October 1940 are a mirror image of this plan. Proposed PWA projects.

Fire Station #2 Warrenville Center Road at Shaker Boulevard, Shaker Heights. Designed August 1938. Two-story Georgian building with a five-bay facade, containing engine room and firemen's quarters. Alternate scheme was made in a more modest Tudor style. Unbuilt.

Monongalia County Hospital Morgantown, West Virginia. Designed November 1938. A four-story addition in the modernistic idiom to an existing hospital. Brick facade with a stone center entrance pavilion and bronze art deco light fixtures. Tucker & Silling, associated architects. A PWA project. Extant.

Jones, Day, Cockley & Reavis Offices 1759 Union Trust Building. Designed November 1938. Alterations and additions to an office suite, with paneled reception room, wainscoting, and furniture designs. Drawings by Dana Clark. For the law firm formerly Tolles, Hogsett & Ginn.

Burrows Brothers Store 633 Euclid Avenue. Designed 1938. Storefront remodeling for space in Guardian Building. Altered.

Competition for a Monument to Jose Marti Havana, Cuba. Designed 1938. A proposed design for a colossal winged figure 48 meters (158 feet) tall, standing on a stepped terrace. Unbuilt.

Port Canaveral Cape Canaveral, Florida. Designed January 1939. Advisors and consultants in charge of plans for developing the commercial harbor of Port Canaveral, with ship channel, wharves, yacht basin, and seaplane base. Unbuilt.

Black River Bridge Erie Avenue, Lorain, Ohio. Designed February 1939. A double-leaf bascule span between piers, the longest such span in the world. Stone operators' towers and sculptured benches. Wilbur J. Watson, consulting engineer. Frank R. Walker, consulting architect. Extant.

The Arcade 401 Euclid Avenue. Designed June 1939. A major alteration of the Euclid Avenue facade, replacing the Romanesque archway with a square red granite entrance, and providing new bronze work to match the existing store fronts. Dan Mitchell in charge. Extant.

William Garrick Wilson Monument Wooded Road, Section 17, Lake View Cemetery, 12316 Euclid Avenue. Designed October 1939. A funereal monument consisting of three cubical masses focused on a sculptured relief panel. Sculpture only executed, with a hovering spirit descending on two angels. Designer: Dana Clark. Extant.

City Club of Cleveland 712 Vincent Avenue. Designed November 1939. Documentation of the structural solutions for building a basement under the existing City Club building. No drawings of the existing building were available. Demolished.

Vincent Barstow Building 522 Prospect Avenue. Designed December 1939. Renovations to the elevators and stairs of an existing four-story nineteenth-century building. Attributed to C. W. Stedman. Demolished.

Rosenblum's Store 321 Euclid Avenue. Designed 1939. Alterations and addition of a third floor to the existing retail and restaurant building (1918). Demolished (BP America site).

St. Lawrence Catholic Church, 1937.

National City Bank Euclid Avenue at East 6th Street. Designed 1939. The addition of colossal Ionic facade columns and alterations to the entry vestibule of the old Garfield Building for National City Bank. Designer: Dana Clark. Unbuilt.

Forest Hills Park Foot Bridge Forest Hill Boulevard, East Cleveland. Designed 1939. Wilbur Watson, engineer; Frank R. Walker, collaborating architect; A. D. Taylor, consulting landscape architect. A concrete arch with a 140-foot span and 48 feet above the boulevard, faced with random ashlar sandstone. Extant.

Buckeye Cycle Building Mill and High Streets, Akron. Designs 1939 for a modernistic facade to an existing building. Building had previously been altered in 1920 by Taylor and Taylor, Canton, architects. Extant. Altered.

Toledo Plate and Window Glass Warehouses 3131 St. Clair Avenue and 3106 Hamilton Avenue. One-story concrete-frame warehouse on St. Clair erected 1939 for lessee U.S. Plywood. Demolished. Alterations to Hamilton Avenue warehouse 1940.

Proposed Apartment Building Washington, D.C. Designed January 1940. Proposed five-story modernistic apartment building with a geometric vertical entrance facade and horizontal banding. Two sites were proposed: New Mexico and Cathedral Avenues, or 16th Street and Shepherd. Unbuilt.

Proposed Apartment Building northeast corner Prospect Avenue at East 46th Street. Designed March 1940. Three-story L-shaped apartment building of nondescript style with thirty-six units per floor. Unbuilt.

Central High-Level Bridge 21st Street and Kansas Avenue over the Black River, Lorain, Ohio. Designed April 1940. Wilbur Watson, consulting engineer; Frank R. Walker, consulting architect. Sketches for 40-foot stepped pylons, bridge approach markers and tablets signed by F.R.W. Pylons unbuilt. Bridge extant.

Portal of Progress Undated. Preliminary conceptual sketches for two monumental sculptured pylons inscribed "Ohio," "Harmony," and "Progress," flanking a six-lane roadway and similar to the Lorain 21st Street Bridge pylons in style. Proposed location unidentified.

Colonial Furniture Company 739 Prospect Avenue. Designed April 1940. Alterations to an existing five-story store building, with modern flat facade except for four glass-block vertical accents, and modernistic light standards. Drawings by Dana Clark. Demolished.

Dairyland Store East 65th Street at Waterman. Designed May 1940. One-story dairy store in the vernacular drive-in style, with a giant rooftop milk bottle in the roadside pop art idiom. For Meyer Dairy Company. Extant.

St. John's Home for Girls Chapel West High Street, Painesville, Ohio. Designed July 1940. Simple brick gable-roofed chapel with a classical entrance of white pilasters and entablature, with side and rear elevations of two stories on a sloping site. Drawings by Dana Clark. Extant.

Universal Film Exchange Building 2340 Payne Avenue. Designed 1940. Alterations to an existing building for RKO Radio Pictures. Demolished.

Building for Frank M. Cobb 11302 Euclid Avenue at Cornell. Designed 1940. One-story commercial building for Marshall Drug. Completed 1942. Extant. Altered.

General Campus Plan, West Virginia University Morgantown, West Virginia. Designed 1940. A proposed university campus plan.

Fairmount Presbyterian Church 2757 Fairmount Boulevard, Cleveland Heights. Designed April 1941. The main sanctuary, in the style of an English village church with a tower and spire, added to an existing 1924 parish house by Bloodgood Tuttle. Constructed of Ohio sandstone. Notable for its stained glass windows. Extant.

Kanawha County Court House Charleston, West Virginia. August 1941. Preliminary studies for a fourteen-story office building containing all of the county functions. Unbuilt.

Adaptive Use Study for Daisy Hill Hunting Valley, Ohio. December 1941. A proposal for the adaptive use of the main residence on the Daisy Hill estate, vacant since the Van Sweringens' deaths in 1935–36. Subdivision plan by F. A. Pease and A. D. Taylor.

Mausoleum for Josephine Forsyth Myers Lot 31, Lake View Cemetery, 12316 Euclid Avenue. Designed 1941. A rectangular private mausoleum with a classical temple front in the Corinthian style. Inscribed "Philip Andrew Myers." Extant.

Proposed Boys' Club Residence Undated. Five-story residence with lobby, lounges, cafeteria, classrooms, club rooms, pool room, and dormitory floors. Probably preliminary proposal for the Cedar Avenue branch YMCA, 1941–42. Walker & Weeks consulted, but Maier & Walsh were selected.

Cleveland Quarries Tramway South Amherst, Ohio. Designed February 1942. Proposed addition and alterations to an overhead crane tramway for moving quarry stone. C. M. Barber, structural engineer.

Julian C. Bolton Residence Kenridge Farm, Mentor, Ohio. Designed April 1942. Alterations to an existing estate, with interior details and garden sketches. Drawings by Dana Clark. For vice president of M. A. Hanna Company and brother of Chester C. and Kenyon C. Bolton.

Bedford Gardens Housing Project Bedford, Ohio. Designed 1942. The complete plan for a proposed federal Defense Housing Project (OH-33073) for the Cleveland Metropolitan Housing Authority, on a 75-acre site between Warrensville Center and Northfield Roads at Talbot Drive. Site plan for administration building, community building, and 160 houses. Drawings by Dana Clark. Unbuilt.

Ohio Farmers Insurance Company Buildings Westfield Center (LeRoy), Ohio. Designed 1943. A group of several buildings for the company's home office, including alterations and additions to the 1835 Westfield Inn, a three-story office building and print shop annex, dormitory building, club house and swimming pool, boiler house and laundry. Unbuilt.

Holy Trinity Polish National Catholic Church 7460 Broadway. Designed 1943. A small sanctuary proposed in both colonial and Romanesque versions. Unbuilt.

United Vacuum Cleaner Stores 1224 Huron Road. Designed July 1944. Remodeling of an existing four-story building (1910) for display, sales, parts, and stockroom. Extant. Altered.

Case School of Applied Science General Plan Designed October 1944. Proposed general campus plan for the development of the quadrangle, with a major building closing the north end of the axis at Euclid Avenue, and new buildings along the East Boulevard flank of the campus.

Harmon Hill Development Ernst Estate, Gates Mills, Ohio. Designed November 1944. Plan for a group of three houses on a portion of the Ernst estate, including one for Tinkham Veale, a long colonial house with a classical stoop and a garage wing. Draftsman: F.R.W.

Bond Store Euclid Avenue at East 9th Street. Designed January 1945. A unique late modernistic building with a circular corner element, solarium, and zigzag walls. Erected 1946–47. Unusual interior space with three-story well. Interior floor planning by Herbert B. Beidler, Chicago, 1944. Demolished 1978.

St. Ann's Parish Church Coventry and Cedar Roads, Cleveland Heights. Erected 1949–51. (See St. Ann's Parish Church, 1928.) Large classical basilican church with a campanile, incorporating materials from the demolished First National Bank on Euclid Avenue (J. Milton Dyer, 1906). Facade with a temple portico and interior hall with Ionic columns, coffered ceiling, and semicircular apse. Dedicated 1952. Extant.

Lutheran Hospital 2609 Franklin Boulevard. Designed October 1945. New brick four-story wing connected to the existing hospital building, with central corridors flanked by operating and patients' rooms. Extant. Altered.

Tomlinson Hall Case Institute of Technology. Designed 1945. Campus social center, with lounges, meeting rooms, and dining facilities. Transitional in design between the classical and modernistic styles, with an unsymmetrically placed entrance block, stylized classical pilasters, and modernistic interiors. Extant.

Davis Plywood Corporation 12555 Berea Road. Designed 1945. A two-story modern office building with horizontal lines and large areas of glass. Not extant.

Army Medical Library Washington, D.C. Designed March 1946. A four-story modern classical building with library, museum, and auditorium. Planned to harmonize with the federal Library of Congress group. Eggers & Higgins, architects; Walker & Weeks, consulting architects. Unbuilt.

Elyria Telephone Company Elyria, Ohio. Designed 1946. Minor structural alterations to main telephone exchange building to accommodate new equipment and accounting department.

Halle Brothers Company Store 1228 Euclid Avenue. Designed 1946–47. Interior modernization, alterations, and addition of three stories to the department store building (1910) by Henry Bacon. Also designed a proposed addition to extend the original building to the point of Huron and Euclid.

    West Wing Huron Road. An eleven-story addition connected to the Euclid Avenue building and bridging East 12th Street.

Service Building Prospect Avenue. A seven-story service, shipping, and vehicle building connected to the Huron Road annex (1926). All buildings extant. Point building unbuilt.

Erie Building Prospect Avenue at East 9th Street. Undated. Probably ca. 1947. Preliminary sketches for alterations to the large corner building, containing stores, storage space, and the Strand Theatre, that housed the YMCA until 1913 and became the Erie Building in 1915. Plans for the Prospect-Bolivar Company. Occupied by Cuyahoga Savings Association in 1947. Demolished.

Dime Bank Building Fort and Griswold Streets, Detroit, Michigan. Designed January 1948. Extensive alterations to the main floor of the twenty-three-story office building (1910) by D. H. Burnham and Company. Alterations to entrances and marquees on both streets in the modern style. Interior alterations for new stores. Building extant.

Cleveland Press Building Rockwell and East 9th Street. Designed February 1948. Alterations to the first floor business offices and second floor offices and lobby of the existing newspaper building (1913). Demolished.

Bill Davidson Residence 58 East Washington Street, Chagrin Falls, Ohio. Designed August 1948. Interior details including fireplace design. Signed F.R.W. Last work signed by Frank R. Walker in the collection. Residence extant.

Russek's Fifth Avenue Store 1101–1109 Euclid Avenue. Designed 1948. A new commercial facade for the existing Stillman Building (1913). A simple, flat, rectangular modern design for the two-story base, leaving original terra-cotta ornament intact above. Building extant. Facade destroyed.

BIBLIOGRAPHICAL NOTES

The PRIMARY SOURCE of information was the Walker and Weeks Collection in the Library of The Western Reserve Historical Society, Cleveland, Ohio. Descriptive materials of the buildings are based on the architectural plans, drawings, sketches, photographs, correspondence, and other papers in the collection. (All cited letters and unpublished papers are found in the collection.) The author visited and personally examined more than ninety of the buildings.

Standard published sources include David D. Van Tassel and John Grabowski, eds., *The Encyclopedia of Cleveland History* (Bloomington: Indiana University Press, 1987); William Ganson Rose, *Cleveland: The Making of a City* (Cleveland: World, 1950); Eric Johannesen, *Cleveland Architecture 1876–1976* (Cleveland: Western Reserve Historical Society, 1979); Mary-Peale Schofield, *Landmark Architecture of Cleveland* (Pittsburgh: Ober Park Associates, 1976); Michael G. Lawrence, *Make No Little Plans* (Cleveland: Western Reserve Historical Society, 1986); *A Pictorial History of Gates Mills* (Gates Mills, Ohio: Gates Mills Historical Society, 1976); and Sara Ruth Watson and John R. Wolfs, *Bridges of Metropolitan Cleveland* (Cleveland: N.p., 1981). Other published sources include newspapers, obituaries, city directories, atlases, and plat books. The biographical information on Frank R. Walker comes briefly from the article in Wilfred Henry Alburn, *This Cleveland of Ours*, vol. 3 (Cleveland: S. J. Clarke, 1933). Both Frank Walker and Harry Weeks are listed in Henry F. Withey and Elsie Rathburn Withey's *Biographical Dictionary of American Architects (Deceased)* (Los Angeles: Hennessey & Ingalls, 1970). The operation of the office is described in correspondence from Charles H. Stark to the author in 1989.

Additional information was received through correspondence with various organizations and individuals, including the Allen Memorial Medical Library; the Alliance Public Library; American House, Inc., of Lima, Ohio; Ashtabula Public Schools; the Atlanta Historical Society; the Barberton Public Library; Berkshire County Historical Society of Pittsfield, Massachusetts; Case Western Reserve University Archives; the Diocese of Cleveland; the Gates Mills Historical Society; the Holden Arboretum; the Library of Congress; The New-York Historical Society; the Ohio Historic Preservation Office in Athens, Ohio; the Ohio Wesleyan University Library; Orange County Historical Museum in Orlando, Florida; James Pahlau, Akron; Drew Rolik, Cleveland; Henry R. Timman, Norwalk, Ohio; and the U.S. Army Corps of Engineers, Huntington District, West Virginia.

The notes indicate only those sources from which direct quotations are included or to which direct reference is made in the text.

NOTES

1. Denny A. Clark, "Some of the Recent Works of Walker and Weeks, Architects, Cleveland, Ohio" *Architectural Revue of the Mississippi Basin* 1 (Summer 1930): 3.

2. Letter, FRW to Walter Smith, City Manager, Wheeling, West Virginia, June 5, 1940.

3. William H. Jordy, *American Buildings and Their Architects,* 4 vols. (Garden City, N.Y.: Doubleday, 1976), 3:344–45.

4. "The Work of Walker & Weeks," *The Ohio Architect, Engineer, and Builder* (Sept. 1914): 12

5. Letter, FRW to Walter Smith, City Manager, Wheeling, West Virginia, June 5, 1940.

6. Letter, Charles H. Stark to the author, Apr. 14, 1989. Stark confirms the fact that Walker was the chief designer in Dyer's firm.

7. "The Work of Walker & Weeks," 12.

8. Claude W. Stedman, description of the Federal Reserve Bank of Cleveland, typescript, n.d.

9. Letter, BD for Walker & Weeks to John Wright, Libby [sic] Glass Company, ca. 1935.

10. "The Office of Walker and Weeks, Architects," *The American Architect* (Jan. 20 1928): 115.

11. Wilfred Henry Alburn, *This Cleveland of Ours,* 4 vols. (Cleveland: S. J. Clarke, 1933), 3:89.

12. "John Huntington Polytechnic Institute," David D. Van Tassel and John Grabowski, eds., *The Encyclopedia of Cleveland History* (Bloomington: Indiana Univ. Press, 1987), 577.

13. *Alliance Review,* May 27, June 15, 21, 30, Aug. 2, 14, 28, 1918, Apr. 2, May 2, 1919.

14. Virginia McAlester and Lee McAlester, *A Field Guide to American Houses* (New York: Knopf, 1984), 392.

15. Henry F. Withey and Elsie Rathburn Withey, *Biographical Dictionary of American Architects (Deceased)* (Los Angeles: Hennessey and Ingalls, 1970), 136.

16. Ruth F. Stone, Editorial Department, Walker and Weeks, "The Central Tower Building," news releases, Jan. 17., June 9, 1930.

17. Edward T. Heald, *The Stark County Story,* 4 vols. (Canton, Ohio: Stark County Historical Society, 1950), 2:165.

18. Ibid., 3:463.

19. John D. Baker, "Anonymity and American Architecture," *Historic Preservation* (July–Sept. 1972): 15–17.

20. Maurice O'Reilly, *The Goodyear Story* (Elmsford, N.Y.: Benjamin, 1983), 47.

21. Eric Johannesen, "A Building Worth Killing For?" *Timeline* 1 (Aug.–Sept. 1985): 42–47.

22. "The Work of Walker and Weeks," 13.

23. Ibid.

24. *Cleveland News,* Dec. 14, 1930.

25. John W. Withers, *A Report of the Survey of Public Schools in Cleveland Heights, Ohio* (Cleveland Heights: Board of Education, 1922), 67.

26. Letter, FRW to William J. Corrigan, Aug. 30, 1942.

27. *Bystander* 2 (July 12, 1930).

28. F. R. Walker quoted in *Plain Dealer,* Oct. 1, 1929.

29. *Plain Dealer,* July 3, 1931.

30. Armen H. Tashjian, "Metal for Exterior Walls of Buildings," *Cleveland Constructor* (Dec. 1931): 6–7.

31. "Some of the Recent Work of Walker and Weeks," 7.

32. *The Indiana War Memorial,* brochure, n.d.

33. Penelope Redd, "Federal Reserve Bank Likened to Treasure Casket," *Pittsburgh Sun-Telegraph,* Dec. 20, 1931.

34. Ibid.

35. Ruth F. Stone, "The Harrison County Court House," typescript, Nov. 21, 1932.

36. Letter, Philip Small to F. R. Walker, outlining proposed press release, June 29, 1931.

37. C. W. Short and R. Stanley-Brown, *Public Buildings: A Survey of Architecture of Projects Constructed by Federal and Other Governmental Bodies Between the Years 1933 and 1939 with the Assistance of the Public Works Administration* (Washington, D.C.: GPO, 1939), ii–iii.

38. *Souvenir of Golden Jubilee, St. Vincent Charity Hospital, Dedication of New Surgical Pavilion* (Cleveland: St. Vincent Charity Hospital, 1917).

39. *Dedication of the Warner and Swasey Observatory* (Cleveland: Case Institute of Technology, 1920), 14–15.

40. Michael M. Partington, "Tribute to a Building," *Bulletin of the Cleveland Medical Library* 22 (Oct. 1976): 70–72.

41. Mary-Peale Schofield, *Landmark Architecture of Cleveland* (Pittsburgh: Ober Park Associates, 1976), 172.

42. Elizabeth P. Kirk, "Severance Hall, Cleveland's Temple of Music," *Gamut* (Spring–Summer 1986): 28.

43. William F. McDermott, *Plain Dealer*, Feb. 6, 1931.

44. Letter, Frank R. Walker to Mary E. Raymond, June 1924.

45. Euclid Avenue Baptist Church, *Historical Sketches: Seventy-Five Years of the Euclid Avenue Baptist Church* (Cleveland: Davis & Cannon, 1927), 130.

46. Ibid., 132, 133.

47. Ibid., 135.

48. Gustav Lindenthal, "Monumental Bridges," *Journal of the Cleveland Engineering Society* 9 (July 1916): 25–26.

49. Wilbur J. Watson, *Bridge Architecture: Containing Two-hundred Illustrations of Notable Bridges of the World, Ancient, and Modern, with Descriptive, Historical, and Legendary Text* (Cleveland: J. H. Jansen, 1927), 17.

50. Wilbur J. Watson and Sarah Ruth Watson, *Bridges in History and Legend* (Cleveland: J. H. Jansen 1937), 223.

51. Lindenthal, "Monumental Bridges," 24.

52. Herbert G. Fices, "General Story on the Great Lakes Exposition," mimeographed publicity release, 1936.

53. "Report of the Jury," *Weekly Bulletin, Michigan Society of Architects* 16 (July 1942): 3.

54. Letter, S. Solomons, Bond Stores, New York, to Elmer Babb, Walker and Weeks, Dec. 18, 1944.

55. Letter, Bishop Joseph Schrembs to Rev. John M. Powers, Apr. 24, 1929.

56. F. R. Walker, "Building Stones," typescript, ca. 1929.

57. Letter, Charles H. Stark to the author, Mar. 26, 1989.

58. "The Work of Walker & Weeks."

INDEX